1

An Inferno Art Studio Book www.infernoartstudio.com
Self-Pubished by Createspace and Ingram Spark
Edited by Shayna Scimeca
Copyright © 2019 by Kayla Koeune and Charles Weisel
ISBN 978-0-5785069-6-8

Roads are for Journeys : Motorcycling through Europe

A Table Top Reader By :
Charlie Weisel and Kayla Koeune

Dedicated to all those who wander.

"Those are not lost who find themselves in the world." Kayla Koeune

CONTENTS

Boulder, Colorado 1.3.16

INTRODUCTION, PLANNING, AND PREPARATION

The idea of this adventure was certainly not a new one, nor was it an original one, but it started to become a reality as I was perusing the travel section of Barnes and Noble, as I do so often. Sifting through the maps, because I love maps, I came across Michelins version of the European road map. It felt as if I had the Holy Grail in my hand, the ultimate in motorcycle adventure. This was not the first time I had held this map in my hand, but it was the first time I felt it pull me to the cash register with a sense of purpose. "This must happen" I said to myself, "the time is now". Elated with my purchase, I skipped across the parking lot like a 6-year-old girl with a new Barbie. Feeling as if I was on top of the world, I immediately sent a picture of the map sitting on my gas tank to Kayla and proclaimed that we were going to Europe. Whatever it took, we were going to make this happen.

The planning and preparation for this adventure was soon in full swing. We had motorcycles to rebuild. Let's be honest, my bike was always a mile or two away from completely falling apart, as I do better job of riding it then I do maintaining it. Kayla's motorcycle was in better condition, but still needed plenty of work. Both of our motors received a full rebuild, as well as a pile of other work including new paint, tires and the

such. Our method of reaching the European coast was far from traditional in classic Charlie/Kayla fashion. My desire to find the most difficult roads possible would leave me buried shoulder deep in the map I had purchased for hours on end. In regards to reaching the European coast and our method of doing so, we had chosen the rather obscure method of crossing the Atlantic. We were going to cross on a German cargo ship. The coordinating of that consumed a fair amount of our time, although we did finally make it happen. The jury is still out as to whether or not it was worth it, but more about that later. We also chose to upgrade a lot of our gear. With the full anticipation of cold and rainy weather we decided to make ourselves as comfortable as possible. Heated, water and wind proof gear was in our future and proved to be worth every penny on more than one cold and wet occasion. Full face helmets were also on our list of upgrades. Having both always used 3/4 helmets, or no helmet at all, we decided that the protection the full face would offer from the cold wind and rain would make our lives exponentially more comfortable, these also proved their worth on more than one occasion. Not that there is anything wrong with a 3/4 helmet, but they do tend to be a little rough on the neck at any sort of speed, especially when riding a bike without any sort of wind protection such as a windshield. Our luggage system would need to be improved as well. My throw-over saddle bags had seen better days, they had been repaired on multiple occasions, and it was time to let them go. Kayla had always used a more bohemian system of simply throwing her gear on the rear fender then using approximately 3000 feet of bungee cord to create some sort of "fail proof" webbing that only she could untangle. We chose a North Face expedition bag to create a single, water proof catch-all that we could easily load and unload. It turns out that this was our one weak point. These bags are not as water proof as they claim which led to the inevitable emptying and drying out of our gear, decorating trees in soggy laundry.

Once our gear and motorcycles were in order it was time to dial in our route. Believe it or not, this is the one part of the trip we left the most unplanned. We have both learned over the years that too much planning in this aspect will lead to disappointment. We simply found key points in Europe that we wanted to see and would let the rest unfold on its own. Paris, Stockholm, Italy and the Swiss Alps would be our highlights, or so we thought, and the roads in between would be decided on the go. Rambling travel, it always leads to the best experiences. With all of our affairs in order it was time to warm up the motors and hit the road, and with that, the adventure was under way.

Boulder, Colorado 10.18.14

Longmont, Colorado 2.15.15

Boulder Colorado 3.16.15

11

Boulder, Colorado 3.20.15

SHAKING DOWN AND STARTING OUT

On so many road trips in the past we have just simply started the bikes and hit the road, but this was different. We could feel the excitement and nervousness in the air as our wheels began to turn. We were embarking on something much grander than we had ever taken on before. The idea that we were literally leaving our home, on our motorcycles, with Europe as our destination seemed almost insane. Most people would simply have had their bikes picked up at their house, shipped to a European destination and then fly to meet them. We are not those people. We chose to ride from Boulder, CO to Wilmington, NC, board a ship, and cross the Atlantic with our motorcycles. In doing so we were able to work out some kinks in our recent repairs and make sure our bikes were reliable enough to be in a foreign country. And kinks there were, plenty of them. In fact, the bikes were probably having more problems than they had ever had. My bike barely ran for the first two hundred miles, which led to a roadside melt down where I proclaimed that we weren't leaving until I found the problem. Luckily, I did, and all was well. Next, my brand-new battery decided it wasn't going to make it past Missouri, though Earth X batteries came to the rescue and drop shipped a new one to Wilmington. The problem was that I had to get from Missouri to

12

North Carolina on an undersized battery
from Wal-Mart that was big enough to
keep the bike running but not big enough
to actually start the motor. Kayla got quite
the workout push starting me who knows
how many times, and began to resemble
a female version of Hulk Hogan. Now
I know it sounds like I was the only one
having issues, but rest assured that Kayla
was having her own set of problems. For
example, in Memphis (an overrated town
I don't feel the need to ever return to),
the train tracks downtown run straight
down the center of the road. This is all
fine and dandy until you need to cross
over said train tracks. Don't be fooled
into thinking that there is a nice smooth
transition across them, in reality, it is not
too far off from having to hop a curb in
the middle of the road. The slippery steal
tracks sit comfortably about an inch or
two above the pavement making it quite
exciting when trying to merge across them.
Unfortunately, when Kayla tried to cross the
tracks won the fight and down she went.
With sparks flying, skin peeling off her
hand, and a massive bruise to her ego she
put on one hell of a show for the patrons
on the patio of the bar this all happened in
front of. Fortunately, with the exception of
a bent shifter peg, no major damage was
done. We decided that Memphis would
be a good place to stop for the night,
since things weren't going too smooth at
the moment. The whole bent shift peg
situation would come back to bite us in the
middle of Georgia. Approaching a stop
light, I see Kayla feverishly searching for
a way to down shift. This wasn't going to
happen. It turned out that at some point
during the previous miles it had decided to
abort mission and jump off, maybe it liked
the area and wanted to stay, who knows?
Regardless, today was not its day to leave
us behind so I went back and scoured
the road for what felt like hours until I

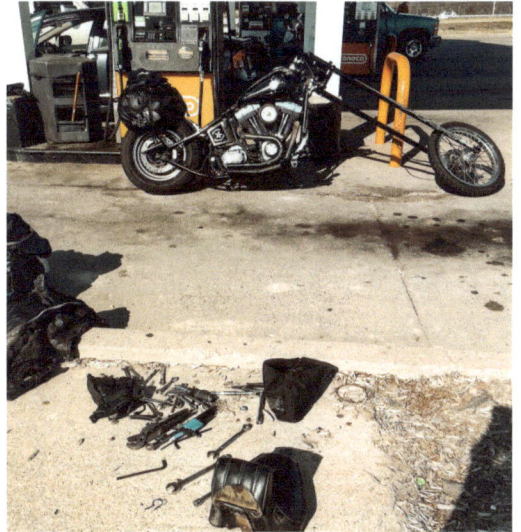

Missouri 3.22.15

Tennessee 3.24.15

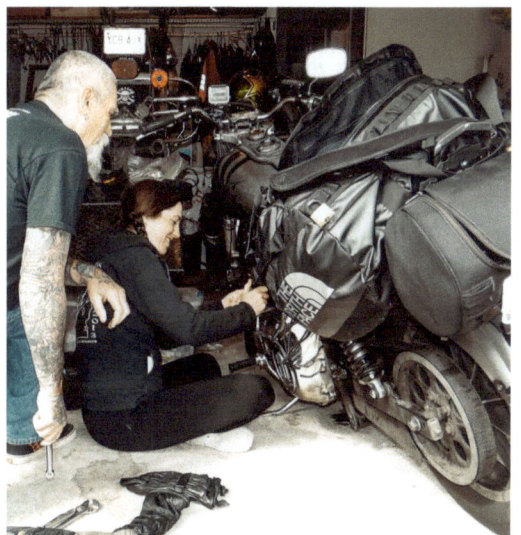

Atlanta, Georgia 3.25.15

13

found it happily lying in the middle of the road. With a smile of success on my face I returned to the gas station and proclaimed that I had saved the day. Unfortunately, the dozens of cars that had chosen to drive over this questionably quality part managed to destroy the shifter peg. As luck would have it a local kid had been watching us curse the situation and offered to help. I cautiously hopped in the kids dilapidated Oldsmobile, wondering if I would ever be seen alive again, and went back to his single wide trailer where we would search through buckets of rusty bolts that would cross thread just perfectly. Again, success was mine. As they say, a cross threaded bolt is a tight bolt. This lobbed together shifter peg sufficed till it could be replaced at mailman's in Atlanta.

Not all of our trip to North Carolina was bad. Along the way we had the opportunity to visit family and friends in Kansas, Alabama, Georgia and South Carolina. Upon our arrival in Wilmington we were greeted by my old neighbors' friend from college. This guy, not knowing us at all outside of a rather distant friend of a friend connection, was generous enough to let us stay with him for the week prior to our ship leaving the port. This became sort of a theme of the trip. Strangers from all walks of life, merely interested in helping us on our journey, would open their doors to us, feed us and wish us luck as we went on our way. A true reminder of how fantastic the human race can be.

I-25, Kansas 3.32.15

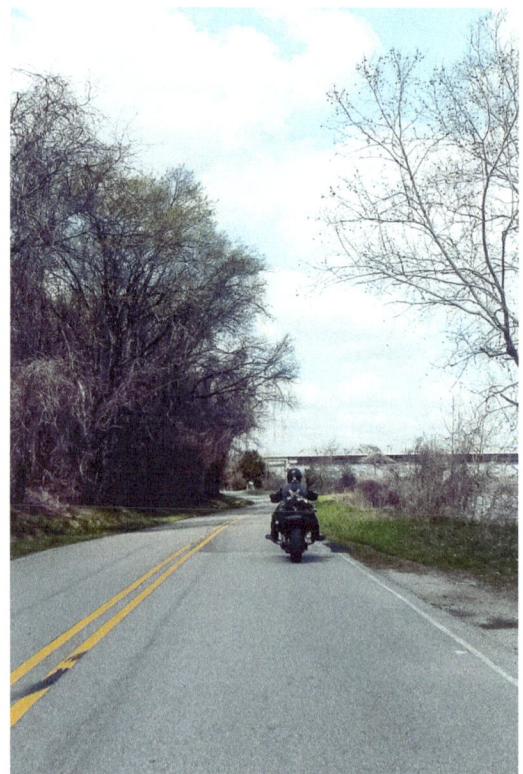

Lacey's Spring , Alabama 3.25.15

14

St. James, Missouri 3.22.15

STROLL TO THE COAST

Phase one, that's what we were calling it. In our minds this was a three-phase trip. Phase one consisted of getting ourselves to Wilmington, NC. Phase two would be the cargo ship ride to Antwerp, Belgium, and phase three would be our adventure in Europe. Why we chose to break down our trip into three parts is beyond me, but that's what we did. Maybe it made it more manageable for us in our heads, I suppose we both tend to over think things. The beauty of choosing to ride to the coast, as opposed to the obviously simpler way of shipping our bikes there, is that it truly made us feel like we were riding to Europe and not just in it. It also allowed us to explore new roads in our home country before exploring new roads in a foreign country. Now, going into this, let me remind you that neither one of us is a stranger to travel. Both of us have covered plenty of ground in the United States, but any possible excuse to explore further is welcomed with open arms. And what an amazing country we live in! Full of diversity, varying landscapes and cultures, the United States truly is a melting pot and one to appreciate.

From Colorado, our ride east would almost immediately dump us directly into the Great Plains. Let's be honest, everything east of Denver is the same until you hit Missouri. This area is considered by most to be boring or drab, but it sort of does something for me. You see, I spent most of my formative years in Wichita, Kansas, an average sized city nestled comfortably right smack in the middle of the Great Plains. This created sort of a love hate relationship with the area. Like most people at the age of eighteen I started looking for a way out, mainly because at that egotistical time in our lives we think our parents are idiots and we want to get as far away from them possible. Usually (as I was), we are proven wrong later in life and realize we should have listened to them more, but this isn't a story about my short comings and mistakes in life, we would need a much larger book for that. Kayla is from the Midwest, Wisconsin to be more specific. Now if you were to compare Kansas to Wisconsin, most people would vote that Wisconsin is a much prettier state, and I would tend to agree. What Wisconsin lacks though, and what I truly enjoy about Kansas, and the Great Plains in general, is the vastness of it. Wide open spaces that seemingly go on forever (Wisconsin has too many damn trees, you can't see more than ten feet). There is a Kansas joke about being able to stand on a soup can and see tomorrow coming, and it's almost true. The sunsets and sunrises are fantastic as well, mostly due to the constant high winds throwing dust in the air. So, you see the Great Plains aren't really all that bad, you just have to change your perspective and try not to fall asleep while crossing them.

Our first stop on the ride would be at my parents' house in Salina, Kansas. Where we would be welcomed with open arms and a warm meal, (my parents are

St. James, Missouri 3.23.15

Salem, Missouri 3.22.15

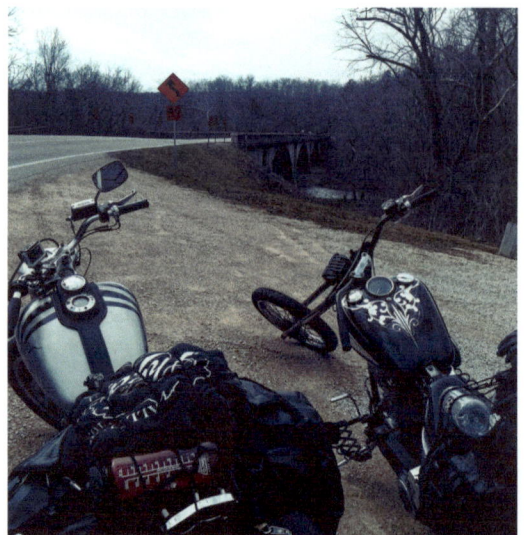

Mark Twain National Forest, Missouri 3.23.15

16

Highway 61, South Carolina 3.26.15

good like that and my Moms meals never disappoint). Not the least bit interested in
motorcycles, or long-range travel for that matter, they always seem to support whatever
hair brained idea I might have, with the exception of a few of them. They seemed a bit
on the fence about this particular adventure but were supportive nonetheless. From
Salina we carried on to Kansas City to spend a night with our friend Wes (always a
welcome sight for sore eyes), and from there we would venture our way to Memphis.
Memphis was an exciting destination for us since neither of us had been there. With the
prospect of world class BBQ, music, and neon lights we rolled into town with more than
mild anticipation. This was going to be fantastic we thought to ourselves, and it was in
a lot of ways. Once we recovered from Kayla's train track mishap (which I talked about
in a previous chapter), we opted to find a swank hotel to hunker down in for the night.
This felt like a much-needed reward after a tough afternoon. We took the opportunity
to clean ourselves up with a warm shower, something we hadn't done in a few nights
(which was apparent by the looks of disgust on people's faces as they walked near us),
and take ourselves out on the town. A stroll down Beale Street was just what we needed
and one that ultimately landed us at BB Kings BBQ and Music Hall. BB Kings might be
one of the most iconic venues in Memphis and it certainly lived up to its name. Working
our way through the hordes of other camera yielding, drunk, and overly excited tourists

we found ourselves a table near the stage in order to ensure a maximum Memphis experience. We were not disappointed. Classic blues music graced our ears at 5000 decibels as classic home style cooking graced our stomachs. Maybe sitting that close was a bad idea. What? Did you say something?

With Memphis in our rear-view mirrors, we set Alabama, and the home of Kayla's uncle, in our sights. Alabama is an odd state, (I'm sure I'll get blasted for saying that), but it is. For whatever reason it always seems to be perpetually a decade behind the times. That being said, I like it for just that reason. I'm sure I'll get blasted for saying that as well, but I sort of like the fact that people in that part of the country seem more focused on living then they are about being politically correct about everything. Live and let live, it is a theme that extreme liberals tend to preach but simultaneously fall short of actually doing. To be clear, no I'm not a hard-core Republican and I'm not intending to launch into some sort of political rant, but I do appreciate the hard-working Americans that don't feel the need to censor every word out of their mouth for fear of offending somebody. Kayla's uncle seems to be the poster child for this way of living, and for that, I really enjoyed his company. If we had more time to spend with him we would have taken it, but alas, it was time to move along and go visit our friends in peach country, Georgia.

He goes by the name of Mailman because yeah, you guessed it, he's a retired mailman. Full of whit and smiles Mailman and his wife Cheryl, are some of the most welcoming people you have ever met. In addition to putting us up for the night he also assisted in the repair of Kayla's shifter peg that had fallen off along the way. That's what Harley's do, they eject parts for no apparent reason, it's amazing that

Charleston, South Carolina 3.27.15

Highway 61, South Carolina 3.26.15

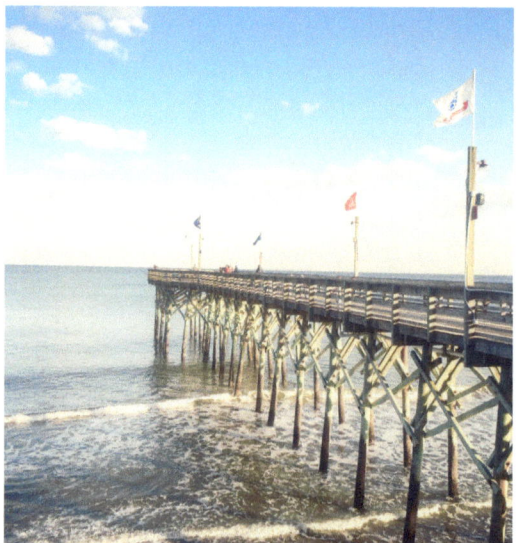
Myrtle Beach, South Carolina 3.25.15

Wilmington, North Carolina 3.31.15

they are still in business. Once the repair was complete we focused more on telling tall tales and eating pizza on the couch. Perfect. The casual exchange of stories with other well-traveled people is one of my favorite past times, and Mailman has no shortage of entertaining stories from a life of shenanigans. The downside to this sort of travel is that there is never enough time to spend with the generous people of the road, and again, it was time to move along.

Charleston, South Carolina was probably our biggest surprise of the east bound trip. Neither one of us expected to be as impressed with it as we were. An absolutely beautiful city drenched in history, Charleston was nice enough to get us thinking about moving there. Kayla's brother is also a resident of this historical town, which prompted our visit. Mike, a bit younger than us, took us on the grand tour. An hour at the piers led us to witnessing a fisherman accidentally hooking a stingray, a walk thru the outdoor market gave us a strong taste of the local flavor and a visit to ancient graveyards reminded us of the not so glamorous side of these Deep South towns, slavery. A staunch reminder of a part of our history many choose to ignore, but we most certainly should not. All in all, Charleston is a splendid town that left a pleasant taste in our mouth, and a return is most certainly in our future. Charleston also proved to be the perfect final stepping stone to the end of our east bound journey. One more stretch and we

19

would find ourselves in Wilmington, North Carolina.

Our ship was set to sail 6 days after our arrival in Wilmington. This was the allotted time for us to prepare our bikes for shipment, get them loaded into a container and say our goodbyes. They would not be seen again until our arrival in Antwerp, Belgium. Our motorcycles are a bit of an extension of ourselves (I suppose more so for myself then for Kayla), which makes it hard to walk away from them. Thoughts of our bikes falling off the ship and into the ocean haunted me until I saw them again. I never liked coral on motorcycles it just isn't my style. Alas, everything went flawlessly and we would soon be reunited. Given as we had 4 days to kill in Wilmington once our bikes were safely tucked into a container, we thought the best way to commemorate the trip would be to get tattoos. We both already have plenty of them so what's one more, we thought. Doing something we don't typically do, we stumbled into a local tattoo shop and inquired about an available artist. At first, they told us they were fully booked (which is a good sign by the way if you are looking for a quality tattooer), but then we explained what we were doing and when we were leaving. After hearing our story, the owner agreed to stay late and take part in our adventure. We discussed ideas for an image and then left him to refine it. What he came up with was perfect. A color accurate globe with a long chopper through the middle of it. Choppering the World, he captured it perfectly.

With our fresh tattoos, butterflies in our stomachs, and motorcycles somewhere in the pile of containers secured to the ship, it was time to raise the anchor and begin our eleven-day Atlantic crossing to Europe. No turning back now as the waves began to gently rock the massive floating freighter, only forward.

Wilmington, North Carolina 3.31.15

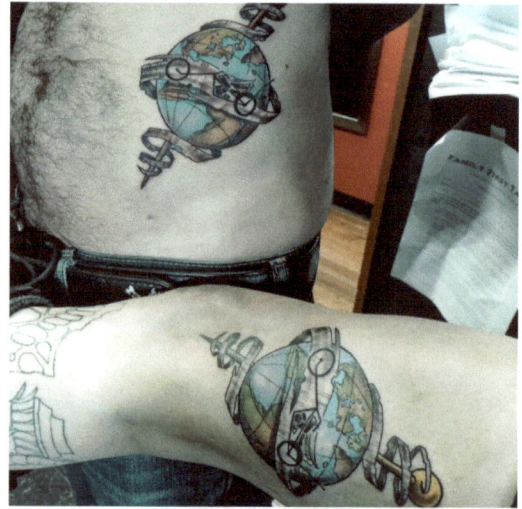

Wilmington, North Carolina 4.2.15

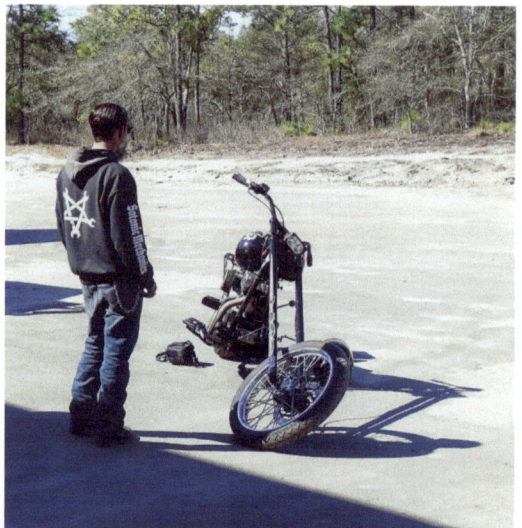

Wilmington, North Carolina 3.31.15

20

Loading of the Ship for the Atlantic Voyage. Wilmington, North Carolina 4.3.15

TRANSATLANTIC CROSSING

It was a bucket list item Kayla and I had both had, to cross the Atlantic Ocean on a working ship, though we didn't know of this commonality until well into our relationship.   In fact, it never really came up until we actually began planning this adventure. I remember sitting with her on the couch and casually mentioning the idea when she profoundly stated that she too had always dreamt of the same. It was from that moment that we solidified our objective to make our way to the European coast by way of water. Now, you have to keep in mind here that neither one of us had any experience in the field of large ships, or extended stays on the water. This meant that we would be embarking on our wavy journey completely blind and not entirely sure how our stomachs would handle the endeavor. Allow me to deviate for a moment though and discuss the logistics of what we were attempting. In our minds we pictured this romantic notion of two adventurers rolling their motorcycles onto a great ship and then sitting with them while gazing across a blue green ocean as seagulls chattered overhead and dolphins leaped rhythmically from the water as if guiding our way. We would lounge on the deck under the warm ocean sun, review maps of the countries we would soon explore and at night we would gaze at the stars while the moonlight cloaked us

Container Ship on the Atlantic Ocean 4.3.15 - 4.14.15

in its nocturnal luminescence. Ah yes, sounds romantic as a day time soap opera, but sadly is a far cry from reality. Yes, our motorcycles were on board the ship with us, but they were stuffed into a container then stacked so deep that who knew where they actually were. Yes, we lounged on the deck of the ship for the first couple of days but then we veered east into the massive swells of the frigidly cold Atlantic Ocean where things began to digress quickly. Sure, we scoured maps and planned our route, but only between my retching in the bathroom from the relentless sea sickness that had reared its ugly head. All this was a harsh reminder that we were on a massive container ship and far from the luxuries and comfort of a fully equipped cruise liner. And the food, well it makes me nauseous even thinking about it. Picture an entire boiled fish, head and all, slapped onto a plate then drenched in oil. Bon a petit! It was painfully clear that the chef (if we dare call the poor mechanic turned cook a chef), had absolutely no idea how to prepare a meal. Apparently, the regular cook was unavailable so they must have flipped a coin to see who would be stuck with the burden of feeding the crew on this particular journey. I pictured him back in the kitchen intentionally creating the most unpleasant concoctions in an effort to insure his place back in the engine room where he belongs and as far from the kitchen as possible. His meals always crescendo with a ladle of oil and a lack of seasoning, leaving even the most adventurous and open-minded eaters questioning his methods. I can tell you with complete confidence that Kayla and I were not alone in this line of thinking as it became a daily discussion as to what mishap would arrive on our plates come feeding time. Surprisingly, the cook managed to actually get worse as the trip went on and we all eventually chose to abandon our attempts at politeness and opt

Captains Deck 4.3.15

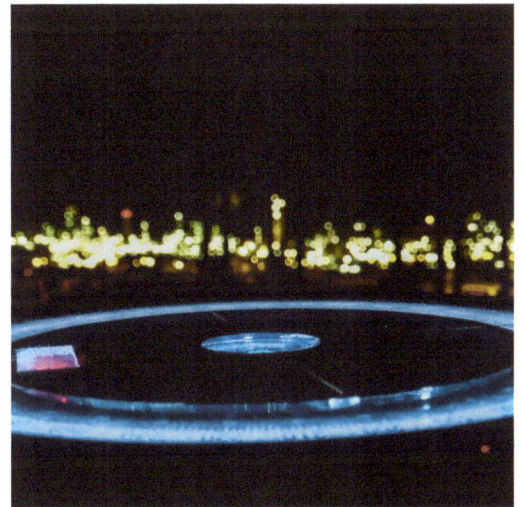
Porthole to the Atlantic 4.5.15

Captains Deck 4.13.15

23

Last Sunset on the Water. English Channel 4.13.15

for peanut butter and jelly sandwiches. Even the ship's captain was appalled, I imagine words were spoken.

I focus on meal time because the reality was that food had become our main source of entertainment. Being as how this truly was a working ship; extracurricular activities were limited to what you could devise on your own. We found ourselves playing Scrabble a fair amount with the other three guests onboard which led to some interesting debates as to what actually was a word and how it was spelled. Turns out that though we all spoke English, there was often variations in spellings between the US, Canada, and England, leading to some borderline heated discussions about which was correct. That's right, three other guests. On board with us, aside from the predominately Polish and Russian crew was a couple from Vancouver and an older chap from England. Five of us in total. We got to know each other very well over the course of our 11-day voyage and had all chosen this obscure method of travel for varying reasons. The Canadian couple had decided that a container ship crossing was the eco-friendliest way to cross the Atlantic. I've yet to do the research on that, but I still find it hard to believe. I suppose that's an argument better left to the experts. The English bloke chose this method of crossing for reasons I can relate to, a total disconnect from the world for eleven days. With no cell service or WiFi connection you are truly forced to focus only on the present. For many of us who have jobs that require constant communication with others via email, cell phones, text messages, and social media, the idea of a total disconnect can be very appealing. When it comes to Kayla and I, we chose the container ship option for simpler reasons, the romanticism. I suppose it was also because it was different, slightly more difficult, and ranked higher up the adventurous scale then simply hopping on a plane. We certainly like doing things in ways most people wouldn't consider, but more than anything it was to get a taste of how travel across the pond used to be. Long, arduous, and secluded.

It was on the tenth day that we saw a bird, this was our cue that we were approaching land, a tell tale sign that sailors have used for years. It's funny how a bird sighting can evoke such emotions of excitement, it's not something a land dweller such as myself thinks about much until you are put in that position. Soon, there was a buzz amongst the five of us about our arrival as we all began scouring the horizon for land. It wasn't long until it was spotted. It would be just a matter of hours now before our feet would be back on soil and my incessant retching would come to end. I think I was more excited about having a calm stomach then I was about reaching Europe.

Looking back on this part of the trip I can tell you that it was truly a once in a lifetime experience, one that we will unlikely repeat. If you have a strong stomach, a longing for seclusion, and a hankering for bad food, then by all means, go for it. If on the other hand you are like me, thoroughly unsuited for the life of a pirate, then I suggest the more traditional method of flying. You will arrive at your destination in considerably better condition, and eleven days quicker. Do I regret our decision to opt for the water crossing? Absolutely not. Though I appear to be focusing on the negative, it was truly an experience Kayla and I would not take back and simultaneously not attempt again.

First meal on the Atlantic 4.3.15

Middle of the Atlantic 4.10.15

Engine Room. English Channel 4.13.15

The Bell Tower of Notre Dame. Paris, France 4.19.15

THE CASTLE BELLS

We are a lucky traveling duo. For the most part, Charlie and I like to seek out the same aesthetics. We tend to gravitate toward roads that take us to the adventures that lie within breathtaking natural phenomena. On this particular trip, we did not discriminate from partaking in our fair share of site seeing. I am a nerd by nature, so being able to glimpse into another culture's rich history had me full with excitement. It is always beautiful to see how the traditions of a past hold strong and continue to mold and shape the present. Charlie and I were prepared with our list of "Must See's," and the rest of what we peered upon would be left to incidental fate. Our plan (like our personalities), was no plan, and where our motorcycles ended up is what our adventure was to be.

In all of our talks there was one city that we were going to without question, Paris. She is one of the greatest centers of art, fashion and café culture the world has to offer. For Charlie, a former cyclist, and I an artist, Paris was one of those places we both desired to visit for completely different reasons. Charlie grew up following the Tour De France making its home stretch down the avenue des Champs- Élysées. Artists of all mediums have flocked to Paris and produced some of the most pivotal movements for generations. This bohemian mecca of art and splendor stole my soul the moment my

26

wheels met the cobble stone roundabouts and pushed me into a dream.

Seeing all this city had to offer would have been exponentially more amazing had we more time, and it not been so exhausting. Don't get me wrong we are both in decent shape but living on the road, being smokers and walking nonstop when we dismounted our steads was a tiring endeavor. On the first night in this fabled city we found a small family run hotel minutes from the Eiffel Tower. We dropped our bikes and our bags and did the natural thing, had a proper Parisian meal with the grand relic in the background. To our luck a wonderful couple from Milwaukee, WI was sitting next to us and struck up a conversation, small world. By the end of the talk they gave us their museum passes that still had a few days left on them, which is called winning! After giving them a grateful farewell, we made our way to the tower. We held hands, carved our initials in the center of a heart like so many before us, while the Eiffel Tower dazzled us with its magical light show as the sun dipped below the horizon. We headed back to our small room overlooking the courtyard and drifted off. This place is what fairy tales are made of.

The alarm came with a thunderous roar screaming to us that if we didn't get moving the lines would be halfway across the city by the time of our arrival. We fueled ourselves with some coffee, croissants and trekked to our furthest destination the Notre-Dame Cathedral. We were in luck, the wait was only about a half an hour to enter the towers, but I feel neither Charlie and I were prepared to Stairmaster the 387 steps to the bells at that hour of the morning. Taking that last step and seeing the complete panoramic view of the entire city and seeing the magnificent craftsmanship of the gargoyles and the massive bells made the sweat effort worth it. We couldn't have

Antwerp, Belgium 4.14.15

Winged Victory of Samothrace. Paris, France 4.19.15

Antwerp, Belgium 4.14.15

Paris, France 4.18.15

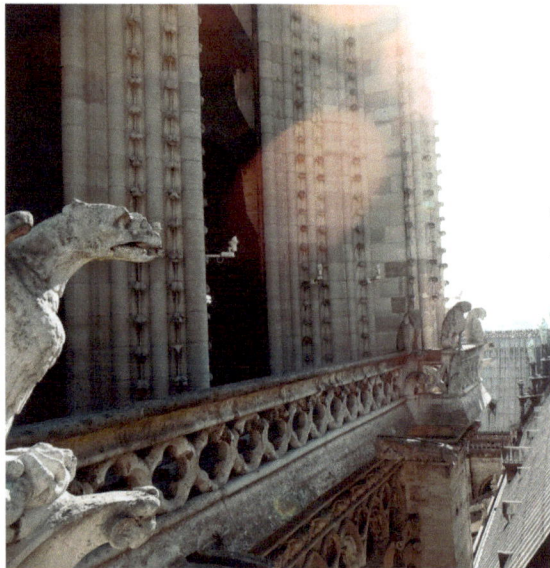

The Bell Tower of Notre Dame. Paris, France 4.19.15

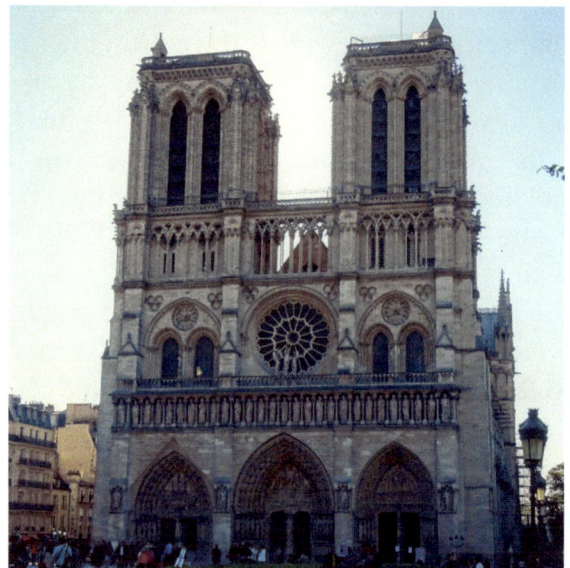

Notre Dame. Paris, France 4.19.15

Illegally Parked. Paris, France 4.18.15

Orangerie Museum. Paris, France 4.19.15

Neuschwanstein Castle. Hohenschwangau, Germany 5.14.15

been more blessed to see this wonder without scaffolding and before the devastating fire. We continued our speed tour by heading to the Louvre to spy the Mona Lisa. I know many comment on her size, but I don't feel size matters, it is the statement made in those eyes and Da Vinci was an architect of emotion. I only wished I could have had one on one time to really look upon his mastery with a closer eye. We wound in and out the halls lined with history and in awe as we made our way across the gardens to the Musée de l'Orangeria. This was the house of Monet's waterlilies, and the masterpieces of other Impressionists of his time. I had no idea how massive and surrounding his work was which was an overwhelming treat. As we exited we were at the precipice of the journey Charlie was dying to make. The long walk down the Avenue Des Champs-Élysées to finish line of the Arc De Triomph. I learned a lot about the Tour de France and cycle racing as we walked to the Arc. Prior to this trip I only knew about Tour de Franzia which is something altogether different. Now after walking to and scaling Notre Dame, the 3.5-mile distance to the Arc de Triomph, and the countless paces taken in Louvre we decided it would be an ingenious idea to hike the 284 steps to the top of the Arc. We took more breaks that I'd like to admit, yet the important part was Charlie's childhood goal was realized. Our feet cried as we made our way back to the hotel, so naturally we had to stop for ice cream to reward ourselves. The next morning, we packed up the motorpickles and continued south.

Another place that put our feet to the test but wasn't on either of our radars

30

was the tiny British country of Gibraltar. Weighing in at a mere 2 ½ square miles, yet packed full of intrigue and historical importance. From atop the quarter of a mile-high Rock of Gibraltar one can see the entire surrounding area to include 3 different countries!! This fact alone made it a military strong hold for hundreds of years, and with over 30 miles of tunnels inside the limestone rock there is no wonder why the British have kept ownership of this real estate. So, without hesitation we hopped in a basket with our friend Amanda who took us to the top and gave us an amazing tour. As we walked down the path we played with the protected Barbary Apes, explored caverns equipped with light shows, peered through old military observation points, and enjoyed some proper Fish and Chips. The part that I still find the most amazing was standing there on top of that rock in one country and with the naked eye peering up the coast to see Spain and gazing across the Strait of Gibraltar at Africa and the Atlas Mountains.

On our journey; we ate the chocolate of Belgium, saw the burros in the hills of Spain, walked through the beautiful architecture of Barcelona and learned of the pride of the Catalan people. I enjoyed drawing while taking in the Mediterranean air at The Château Royal de Collioure. Then it was time to go completely out of our way to Füssen, Germany to find one of my childhood dreams, the Neuschwanstein Castle. For those of you who don't know this is the real-life castle that inspired the Disney Castle specifically found in Sleeping Beauty. The Neuschwanstein stands a white pearl cradled in the side of a mountain that glows while a dense forest that surrounds her. We rode up to the castle gates, but the lines to enter were overwhelming so we went to our campsite and gazed from afar. I completely regret not going in, so maybe there will be a second visit in our future.

Arc de Triomphe. Paris, France 4.19.15

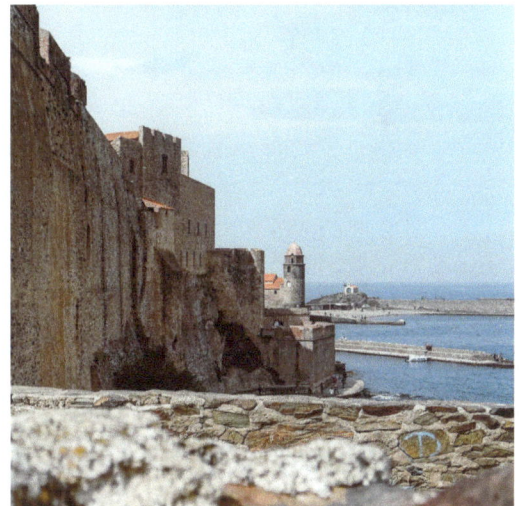
Chateau Royal de Collioure. France 5.4.15

The Eiffel Tower. Paris, France 4.19.15

31

The final city we really took the time to visit before heading back across the pond was Amsterdam. We had several days to roam this metropolis of entertainment. Our friend Mario was amazing with recommendations as well as opened his home to us. A small train ride and we were headed to the heart of the city. I was dying to see the Rembrant's at the Rijksmuseum. He has been my favorite painter since I was young, and although I have seen his pieces in person before I try to never miss a chance to see his work. A man after my own heart as he was a realist who mastered the use of chiaroscuro. This elegant use of shadow and light was a huge influence on my earlier work once again convincing myself I was born in the wrong era. Seeing the massive "Night's Watch" was a real treat. We spent most of our time in Amsterdam recovering from a long journey, making our way through shops, eating all sorts of treats, and taking in the general splendor. Many people told us not to miss the dynamic of the Red-Light District. I feel it is a natural curiosity to peer upon something that is taboo and illegal in your world, yet acceptable and supported in another's. The whole scene seemed so natural. Mothers and grandmothers pushed their infants in strollers through the streets lined with prostitutes in the windows like puppies waiting to be taken. I'd be lying if I said we didn't get turned on by the whole experience, there is something exciting about the openness of sexuality. This was the end of the line of tourism for this trip, and what an interesting finale it was.

Collioure. France 5.4.15

Mona Lisa. Paris, France 4.19.15

Geneva Creek Park. Grant, Colorado 9.20.15

CAMPING, CRASHING, AND HOTELS

There is a dance involved in the artistry of setting up camp in a way that provides more than just shelter for a night. It is the unlashing and unzipping of bags, the moment when things appear to be strewn about in a haphazard manner but yet is simultaneously entirely orchestrated and thought through. Without a word spoken between Kayla and I, a bit of magic happens. Each of us well practiced in our roles to provide an instant home. As I toss the tent in a suitable location, agreed upon with no more than a nod of acceptance, Kayla unfurls the corners while I click together the polls. Together we work seamlessly to raise the tent. The race to see who can inflate their sleeping pad for the night is well underway as we both blow frantically into our pads, without passing out, only to hear "I win!" from that day's champion. With our freshly located shelter in place the dance carries on until every last detail has been deemed complete. The coffee pot has been placed within arm's reach of the tent, along with two mugs, so that in the morning we can enjoy a warm cup of Joe from the comforts of our sleeping bags. Our cooking pot, along with the small camp stove and that night's meal of choice is resting neatly in whatever place we've decided to call the kitchen. Pillows have been placed on the uphill side of the tent. With the set up complete the more

Road to Lichtenstein. 5.13.15

Antwerp, Belgium 6.1.2015

The Room on the ship. Atlantic Ocean 4.3.15

unglamorous side of moto camping begins, especially if there was any rain involved that particular day. Often you will see our neat little camp quickly turn into what looks more like a Hobo Village. Our damp and smelly clothes get strung from every imaginable place possible. Tree branches, fences, our motorcycles, and even the top of the tent. Quite literally anything that can be used as a clothesline is now littered with tired and smelly motorcycle gear.

This is the part of moto travel not often portrayed in those well thought out photographs so proudly posted on social media sites. With the perfect filters, lighting, that thoughtful gaze into the distance, and a motorcycle always parked neatly on the side of a magical road, one would be led to believe that traveling on two wheels is nothing but rainbows and unicorns. Rarely do you see a picture posted of a campsite with a pair of dirty skivvies hanging off the handlebar. The reality though, is that this is more often the case then not. So why do it then? Why go through this daily routine of packing and unpacking then packing again? Why deal with the headache of such things when there are plenty of hotels to be had? For the love of sleeping outside and under the stars is the most common response you will hear, it's more than that though. It's for the love of hearing the crickets chirp, a cool breeze rustling the leaves overhead, the sound of the first singing bird in the morning. This is why we do it. It is the pride in knowing that you have the ability to be self-sufficient, that you have the confidence in knowing that four walls and roof are not a life necessity. It is the comfort in knowing that everything you need to survive is stowed neatly on the back of your motorcycle.

When it comes to the topic of what is needed to survive vs what is simply a creature comfort you should prepare yourself for a wild debate. We did learn

Oberkirch, Germany 5.17.15

Faro, Portugal 4.27.15

Serpa, Portugal 4.27.15

35

Oosterde, Belgium 4.17.15

very quickly for example that our failure to bring camp chairs was a huge mistake. Not that sitting on the ground is the end of the world, but a cozy chair at the end of a long day sure makes for a pleasant way to spend the evening. Why we did not bring chairs with us is still a mystery, I think at the time we were packing we decided that they took up too much space, even though they make them incredibly small these days. From that trip on, the camp chair has moved off of the creature comfort list and onto the necessity list. There is one thing in particular that we did take with us, that was, and forever will be, on the basic life survival list. The one item that will truly make or break a camping experience and could very well save your life. Ok, I may be exaggerating a bit, but we do think that having a cribbage board is a necessity. Kayla and I have spent more nights then I can count hunkered down in our tent, wrapped up in our sleeping bags playing cribbage under the light of a headlamp. For those of you that have no idea what cribbage is, it is a card game that is typically accompanied by a board with 121 holes drilled into it and two pegs per player. The idea is to move your peg down the lane of holes based on your hand played. For us, these nights in the tent playing cards are some of our most memorable, and have proven to be a great way to end a day. If a light rain is providing a subtle pitter patter background on the roof of the tent then that is a just a bonus. I've found over the years that the best sleep I will ever get is laying in a tent on a

36

rainy night.

Some nights though the rain is just too much to tolerate, especially when it is raining while trying to get set up. The logistics of raising a tent in a downpour and managing to keep the inside of it dry is nearly impossible, and a challenge we often pass up. Because of this we tend to lean on hotels when the weather isn't cooperating. Although a hotel is not our preferred method of spending our night it does offer many distinct advantages and comforts. For example, showers. A hot shower after back to back days on the road and multiple nights sleeping outside is approaching a heavenly experience. Soaking in the warm water, letting it soothe your achy bones and tired muscles while washing away the filth of miles upon miles of road grime is a sure-fire way to rejuvenate the body and soul. Follow that up with a good night's rest atop a soft mattress and full-size pillows and a person is almost guaranteed to feel better the following morning. Something else we really enjoy about hotels is that they are typically located in a metropolitan area which gives us the opportunity to explore the local cuisine. These are the nights, that after we clean ourselves up and put on our one non-riding outfits that we enjoy sitting down to a nice meal and allow ourselves to be pampered for the night. We are both firm believers that a day or two of pampering here and there is an essential element to prolonged travel. Without it we feel like it is easy to get physically rundown and mentally burnt out. Motorcycle travel after all is not an easy or simple endeavor and should be rewarded from time to time. In addition to the self-indulgent experience of a hotel and its proximity to quality restaurants, they also open up the option to spend an extra day or two in whatever city we may find ourselves in and sight see on foot. Sometimes spending a day or two on foot is a nice reprieve from the motorcycle,

Le Prese, Switzerland 5.12.15

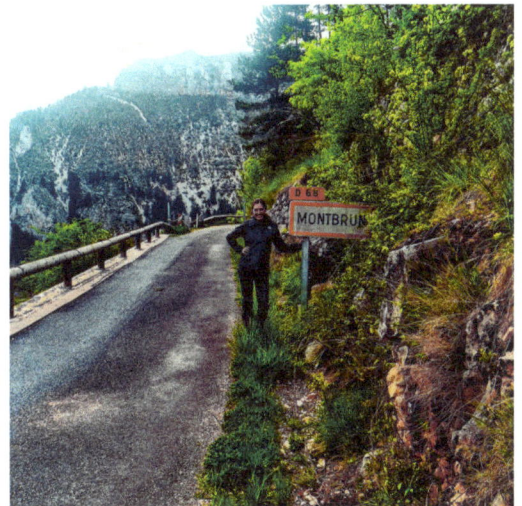
Camping les Osiers. Montbrun, France 4.22.15

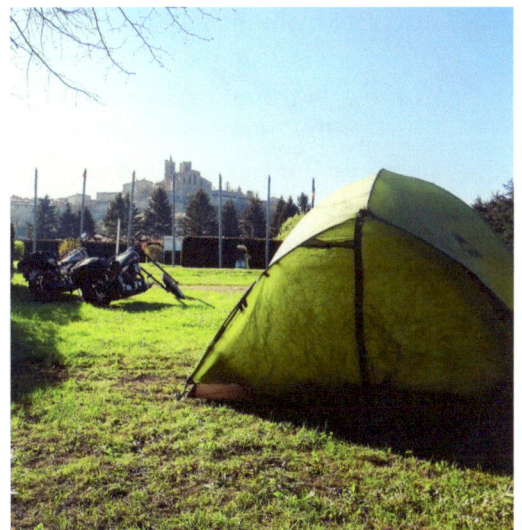
Saint Bonnet le Chateau, France 4.23.15

Gas Station Club House. Flourence, Italy 5.8.15

allowing us the ability to stretch our legs and get the heart pumping. Not to mention the fact that in a lot of cities, Paris for example, most of the major attractions are within walking distance of each other and dealing with parking and busy streets would simply detract from the experience.

Crashing, couch surfing, or whatever you decide to call it is a third fantastic way of overnighting. We enjoy it for a multitude of reasons but one of the biggest draws is the ability to personally connect either with someone new or someone you've known for a while but rarely get to see. With the invention of social media, meeting people from literally all over the world has become easier than ever. Nearly the moment we began posting our travel plans on Facebook and Instagram we started receiving offers for places to stay all over Europe from people we had never met face to face. One of these people was an Italian named Bob and his Chopper club appropriately named Mekka of Choppers. Bob and I had previously conversed over the internet before our trip plans came to fruition solely because we shared a love for the same style of motorcycle. Long, low and fully rigid. For months, while I was building my bike, we discussed the details involved in making them the proper way as to maintain handling and durability. By the time we decided to make the voyage across the pond I knew immediately that a night at their clubhouse was a priority. We were not disappointed with this decision, nor have we ever had regrets for couch surfing anywhere. The clubhouse they built was one of the nicest I have ever seen, complete with a shop area for building and repairing motorcycles, showers, a living room for hanging out, and a bunk house for sleeping. We arrived late and well after dark, this was the same day as Kayla's massive oil leak, man can a lot of things happen in a day. In true Italian fashion they opened their space to us and made us feel completely at ease. This is the beauty of crashing, the realization that the hosts are as excited about you joining them as you are about having a place to stay, and a friendly smile greeting you at the door. We spent the evening with them sharing stories from the road, indulging in authentic Italian pizza followed by a much-needed nights rest. The following morning, we woke to the aroma of freshly brewed espresso waiting for us and a view of the countryside we were unable to see the night before. This of course offered the opportunity for the quintessential Chopper line up photograph in front of the clubhouse, an image I still cherish to this day.

As you can tell, there are many ways of going about closing one's day, each with their own unique sets of pros and cons, with no option better than the other. The key is to find what works for you in that particular moment, and simply enjoy it. We have found that mixing it up works best for us, letting each day unfold naturally and literally letting the road, weather, and opportunities present themselves and do the deciding for us.

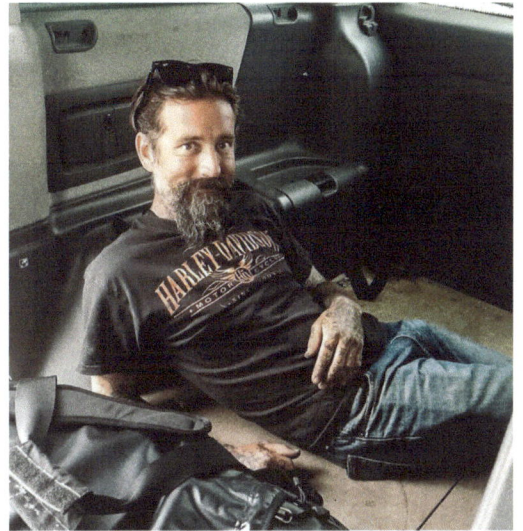

Montpellier, France 5.5.15

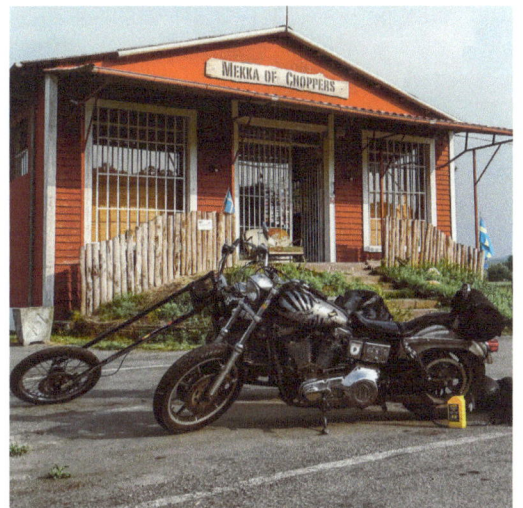

Mecca of Choppers Clubhouse. Italy 5.7.15

Tarazona, Spain 4.24.15

39

OIL DISASTER OF 2015

Motorcycle travel comes with a unique set of difficulties mainly because they are always breaking, or leaking, or parts are just plain falling off. It's part of the adventure of exploration on two wheels. We always tell ourselves fixing motorcycles and trying to keep them on the road is part of the fun. I mean really how exciting are stories where everything goes fine with no issues, and the bike ran like a dream in the afternoon sun. Although we had some afternoons with sun the bikes ran... well... I suppose they ran like heavily used bikes do. Charlie mentioned in an earlier chapter a few kinks we had shaking down the bikes while heading to the coast, but the issues did not stop there. We hit a couple of serious issues that were near show stoppers. Like for real, Charlie and I were entertaining the logistics of riding two up on his bike, or just buying another motorcycle to finish the trip.

The bikes were riding pretty smooth for the most part until we got to Collioure, France... wait what am I talking about, Charlie's pinion gear was on the fritz and about once every 10 starts I had to push start him, run back to my bike, hop on, and catch up to him. It was absolutely ridiculous! The thing was shredding the gear and wouldn't engage properly no matter how hard he worked on it, but that's a story for a different chapter. The true culprit that started a shit show and the near demise of my motorcycle was a garage with a tall speed bump thing at the entrance. Dynas have "great" engineering where they put a completely exposed oil drain plug on the bottom of the bike. Well as I rolled over, the speed bump met the plug causing the oil disaster of 2015, as I like to call it. Now we didn't notice there was a problem till we went to leave Jean's house and saw the pool of oil that had grown beneath my bike. I thought that seems odd. I felt the bottom of the bike a little wet but oil wasn't running out so I didn't give it too much of a thought. A little side note, the plug that I installed in Memphis after I wrecked was an oversized plug that gradually gets fatter the more you screw it in. The helpful thing about it is that it will self-tap and plug the wear in the threads. But the speed bump cracked the drain hole enough to make the plug useless.

Once we started heading down the road, and the oil warmed up, a decent leak started going. It wasn't the end of the world, but it was starting to get worrisome so we started hunting for a shop. The first motor repair shop we found was in Montpillier, France they were geared toward sport bikes but they attempted to help. To give them props they made a valiant effort in fixing the bike. They even brought in a welder and let us sleep in their van overnight outside their shop, so that was cool and little weird. We were also trying to communicate through Google translator. I didn't speak French and they didn't speak English coupled with me being a girl, I would say there was a slight reluctance to hear was I was trying to explain. A guy came in to weld and add material to the drain hole and it looked like there was some hope to moving on. The difficulty is that there was oil everywhere, and welders don't really like to work on oiled metal. He eventually got some metal to build up and then we got to reinstalling

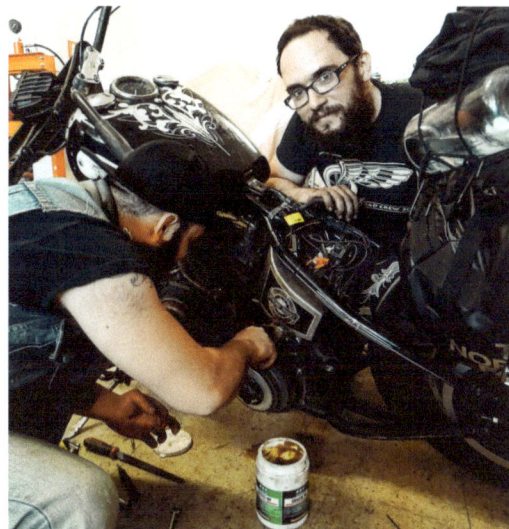

Beard Cycles. Florence, Italy 5.10.15

Antwerp, Belgium 5.31.15

Eindhoven, Netherlands 5.30.15

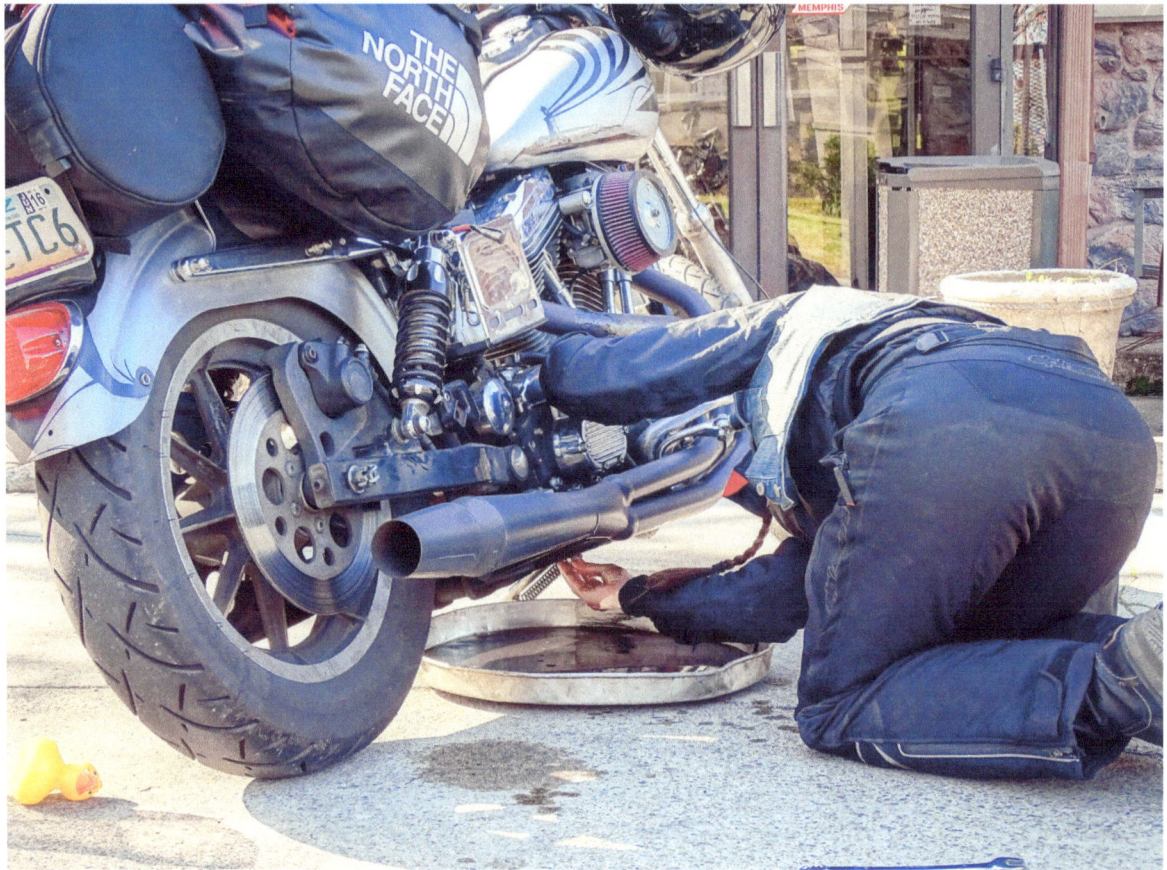

Memphis, Tennessee 3.24.15

the drain plug. I was trying to tell them the nut get fatter the further in you twist so once you feel it snug you need to stop. Well they did not stop and all we heard was a metallic click of doom. That echoing sound of disaster was the oil pan cracking. We needed to start heading down the road, they were out of ideas and we were running out of patience because we were trying to make it to a chopper party in Italy. So, they put some silicon on the crack and off we went.

The temporary fix, as suspected did not last long, and the once smallish leak was now a geyser. I was literally puking a quart of oil every 30 miles and that's being generous. Now if you do some math, that means a metric shit ton of oil is spraying out the bottom all over the rear tire which at this point was just drenched. This led to me having a meltdown, crying and shaking at a fuel stop terrified to get back on my bike. Charlie convinced me he's seen worse (which I would find out months later was a complete lie) and it would be just fine, we will just go slow. Speed doesn't really matter when you're riding on an oil slick.

Thanks to modern technology and social media a friend who had been following our travels contacted us. He gave us the information for the MHC Workshop in Marseilles and said if they can't help no one can. I had no choice but to pull up my big girl pants, add another quart of oil, and wipe down the rear wheel the best I could. A couple terrifying hours later we found the shop on a steep downtown alley. Exhausted from stress I parked my bike just in time for it to lose the rest of its oil on the sidewalk. Roman Vaugnoux, a custom motorcycle builder and fabricator, was a godsend. He had a machine shop that gave me some hope that our trip wasn't over. He pretty much made a plug and welded the whole bottom closed (I didn't need to change the oil anytime soon anyhow.) For good measure he covered the whole welded area with JB weld, because although the weld looked good he was also welding on metal covered from oil. I will let you know that the bike never leaked again. We tried to pay him but Roman charged us just for the oil. Overcome with tears of joy, and a new friend, Charlie and I got on our bikes in time to meet up with the Italians. It was a late start with a few hundred miles to go but we dodged a massive bullet.

There were a few more bumps and bruises along the way. Push starting Charlie was really starting to get old but at least once we got him running it was not dangerous for him to be on the bike. His bike also never really stopped leaking transmission fluid. It was pretty much a constant cycle of adding fluid, and the bike immediately rejecting it back onto the pavement. I also feel there has to be the honorary mention of Charlie running out of fuel on a freeway exit in the pouring rain. Which made me sick with laughter until I realized I would have to find fuel and sacrifice my favorite Nalgene bottle to get him gas to keep going.

The beauty of all of this is our resourcefulness, determination to stay on the road, and the genuine kindness of others which was tested around every corner in order keep us going. We couldn't have done it without the people we met along the way. I also want to sincerely apologize to the South of France for causing a biohazard all along their road ways-that was extremely inconsiderate of me.

Montpellier, France 5.6.15

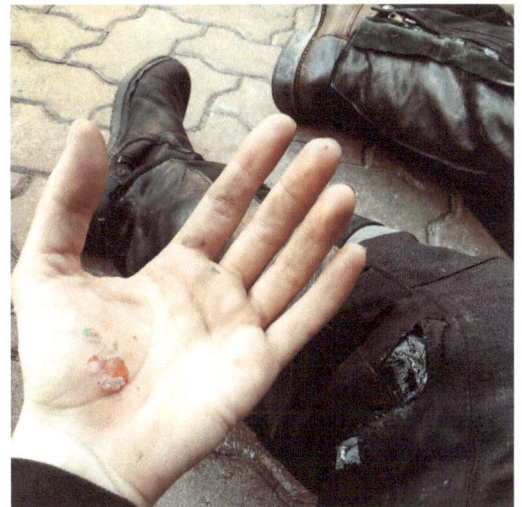

Memphis, Tennessee 3.23.15

Marseille, France 5.6.15

43

Mecca of Choppers. Alba, Italy 5.7.15

THE FAMILY YOU MEET

Traveling is not all about the places you see. The scenery, the climate, and the roads are a big part of that without a doubt, but what travel is really about for many is the people. The people along the way that teach us about their culture, the food they eat, and the way they live on a day to day basis. The people are the ones that stop to help when we are lost or broken down on the side of the road. They are the ones that contribute to the everlasting memories that we will cherish forever. The friendships built in a matter of moments yet last a lifetime.

Traveling by motorcycle, I've learned over the years, dramatically increases your chances of meeting the locals along the way. Just the sight of a motorcycle, heavily laden with all the necessary camping equipment, clothing and tools insights a curiosity in most people. We are viewed as the road warriors, the ones that pay no attention to such comforts as radios, climate control and plush leather seats. We are the ones doing what most people only dream of, but not dare tackle themselves. These are the reasons why most people can't help but wander over and say hello, the classic line of questioning soon following. Where are you going? Where have you been? What do you do when it rains? Some motorcyclists, who often lean more to the introvert side of the spectrum, find this frequent interaction to be annoying after a while. Kayla and I however, use it as an opportunity to learn about the area and about the local heritage. Often times these conversations will be brief, but other times you quickly find a common thread with this stranger, immediately becoming a friend. On more than one occasion I've been directed towards a fabulous place to camp for the night, I've been offered a warm bed and a hot meal, a backyard to camp in, or a local shop that can assist with repairs. I've been offered garage space and tools to make oil changes, rides to a motorcycle shop to buy parts, or simply a bottle of water to cool me down on a hot day. It is the strangers along the way that provide the material for a good story and I firmly believe that they should be heard.

Without a doubt there were a few standout experiences that will stick with us forever. One of those being a fellow named Jean along with his wife and daughter. For a month before we even arrived in Europe he had been telling us that we had to visit him and his family in Collioure, France. We of course took this as a nice gesture, as we had with the many other offers such as this that we had received, and took a mental note to keep this option open. As our journey through Europe took us within a day's ride of Collioure he became more and more adamant about us visiting, and because of that we agreed to it. Unbeknown to us, Collioure, the reason why Jean was so insistent we come visit, is an absolute gem of a town. Before our arrival to this tiny village it was simply a dot on the map, but within moments of our arrival our eyes were opened wide to the magnificence of what we were about to experience. Nestled perfectly on the shore line of the Mediterranean, once protected by a grand castle overlooking the water and literally in the middle of town, Collioure will incite both the romantic and explorer in virtually

Jean. Collioure, France 5.3.15

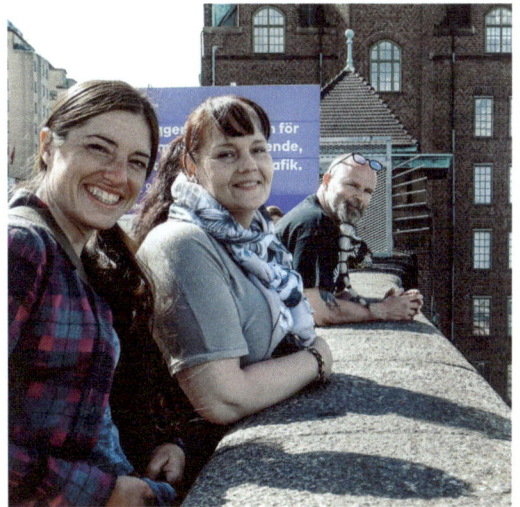
Sussi and Richard. Stockholm, Sweden 5.24.15

Jens. Worth am Main, Germany 5.20.15

Olivier. Macon, France 4.21.15

everyone. In addition to its 17th century architectural charm, the people of Collioure were equally as charming. Jean opened his home to us, made us fantastic meals and even offered us their own bed. The hospitality was beyond anything we've ever experienced. By day we would stroll the narrow cobblestone streets, sit by the water and write, or simply find a bench to relax on while enjoying a scoop of fresh gelato. These are the experiences most often discovered in dreams, but can also be found in Collioure, France.

This was simply one of many experiences we had like this. You can add to that the numerous smaller gestures, such as the family at a campground in Germany we met while they were there for a family reunion, and we were staying there an extra day to wait out the rain. They saw that we were relatively stuck at the campground due to the weather, and being on motorcycles doing simple things such as going for food was a soggy pain in the neck. In light of all this they essentially took us in and invited us to spend time with them indoors to conversate and enjoy a meal together. The following day they even invited us to drive with them to a nearby suspended walking bridge that many of them wanted to see, an invitation we definitely did not turn down. Again, this is a great example of strangers helping strangers. They could very well have just ignored the two soggy bikers hiding out in their tent but instead they chose to bring us into their family, if even for only a couple of days.

I could go on and on like this citing one example after another, but I think we can all agree that these are two good examples of the basic kindness that most people have in them. Too often we get cynical of the direction the world feels to be heading, as people seemingly become less aware of others around them. But I don't believe that view point to be entirely accurate. I still believe that most people truly want to help others, they get excited at the opportunity to show you where and how they live, and share their beliefs and ideas with others. I'm not sure that people are becoming less willing to be open with strangers but that people are becoming less willing to stop and listen. I have said it a million times and I will say it a million more, for those willing to step out their front door into the unknown, to see beyond the town sign and leave their fears of travel at home, the world, and the people in it, will take care of you when things feel dire. When your vehicle breaks down in what feels like the middle of nowhere a truck will come along and offer help. When you are stuck under a shelter hiding from the rain, a stranger will offer a break in the clouds, and when the loneliness of the road begins to creep into your veins, a local will open his doors and take you in. The people you meet on the road will stay with you forever, even if your paths cross for nothing more than a moment. They are unspoken angels that help us weary travelers stay the path and continue on our journey.

Amanda. Gibraltar 4.29.15

Mario. Amsterdam, Netherlands 6.6.15

Mailman. Atlanta, Georgia 3.25.15

Lourve. Paris 4.19.15

THE ART OF HAVING FUN

Adventuring can't always be a relentless endeavor into the great unknown. The nonsensical pursuit of childish joy is essential in rounding out serious travel into pure enjoyment. It's a big deal to step out of one's shell and into the world with true silliness in the wake of the judging eyes of onlookers. There is a nagging feeling to care what they are thinking, although you consistently tell yourself that they are jealous and wish they were having as much fun as you. Then there is that beautiful moment when the desire to be your quirky, weird self outdoes the need to be accepted, and a free awakening of pure enjoyment happens.

This is an aspect of travel that Charlie and I sometimes struggle with. Of course, around the people we know the best in this world our personalities are at full volume, and we are our typical freak show, but in front of strangers… that is a whole other story. We both become pretty shy in public, easily embarrassed, and if one squinted hard enough they may see us hiding behind our mother's leg. This is something we are both working pretty actively on rectifying and many times Charlie takes a bit more coaxing to let it all hang out…. so to speak.

"Ok Charlie, give me a big smile… maybe a thumbs up…anything... oh your giving me a serious face… please... pretty please give me a smile… I will tickle you in public and I'm not joking… THERE IT IS!!!". He can be quite shy, yet I believe it is a

Body Guards. Amsterdam, Netherlands 6.5.15

Mourao, Portugal 4.26.15

Bogense, Denmark 5.21.15

Amsterdam, Netherlands 6.5.15

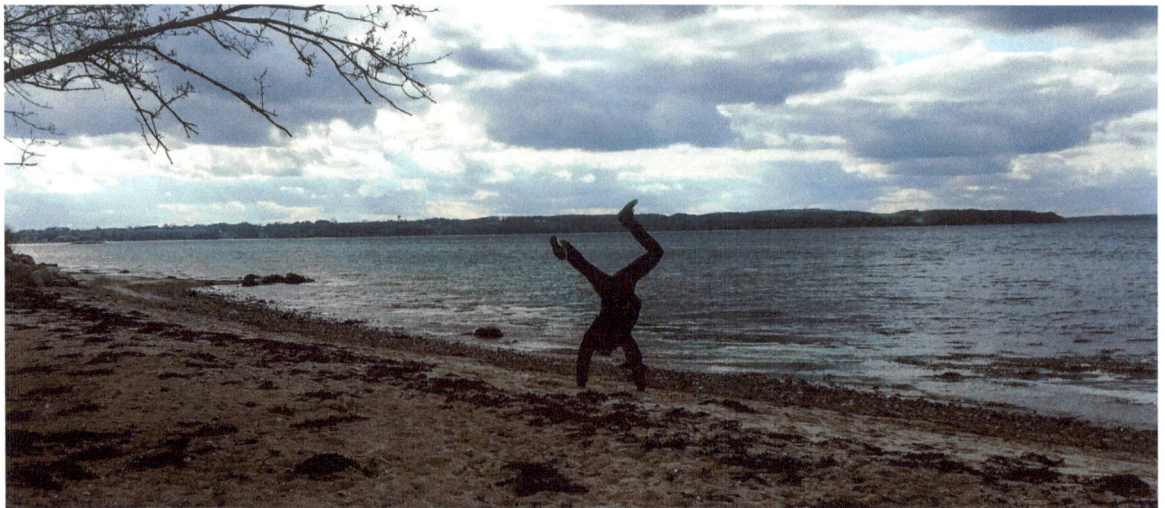

Bogense, Denmark 5.21.15

deep lingering desire to be accepted by others that pushes away the youthful bliss that resides within us, and yearns to be set free to play.

After years together, this need to be presentable on a social level has become less and less of an issue and letting go without the booze has become our goal. The key for most to let go is getting wasted, but seeing as though neither of us drink, we need to rely on our balls to lose our inhibitions. Most of the time spent on a motorcycle is spent in deep contemplation, a therapeutic mental state if you will, so I feel it is important to jump out of that mindset and have some lighthearted fun. You start getting old and increasingly boring when you don't allow yourself to have amusement. How can we not joke at ourselves in this environment? We regularly pulled up on our all too loud for Europe motorcycles, to a nice restaurant or hotel covered in road grime, (and smelling a touch worse), with people staring at you not completely sure how to place you. But our redeeming quality was those American plates, as the distance traveled gave understanding to our visual state as scumbags… which we are… but a little less scary when one realizes we are currently living an adventure on the road. Getting over ourselves helped us to start taking the tourist photos, you know the kind I'm talking about… Cartwheels on the beach, big cheesy grins in front of the country signs as you crossed another milestone boarder, trying to take a picture larger than life with your finger touching the pinnacle of the Louvre yet epically failing, clown cars and silly faces in front of serious art. Although one must partake in adulting here and there I will forever be a wild child, a lost boy… well a girl, but you catch my drift. I guess with all of this all I'm saying is get out there and have fun, and screw the rest.

Bogense, Denmark 5.21.15

Amsterdam, Netherlands 6.5.15

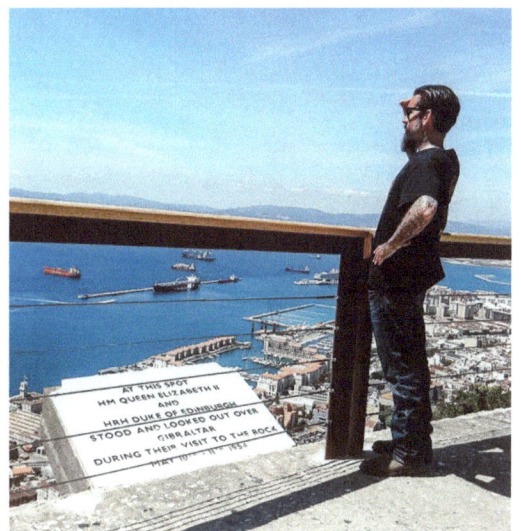
The Rock, Gibraltar 4.29.15

51

Andorra, Andorra 4.24.15

THE NEWBIE

A smile of determination stretches across my face as fear glares my sight. I try to tell my hands to relax as I clench the throttle, but… well… they do what they want. I lean forward attempting to focus on the narrow, water-soaked road filled with potholes and steep drop offs, but my confidence wanes. With each vehicle that whizzes towards me I have a small stroke, because at this point I can barely make them out through the fogged-up lens of my helmet. I scold myself "who is the idiot that removed my perfectly good windshield and front fender?" they really would make a world of difference at this current moment. To top it all off and to add a little salt into the wound Charlie is slowly creeping further… and further… and further from me, not to mention I'm pretty sure there are about 50 cars lined up behind me. How did he get so far ahead? Damn…. He rides so fast and with such ease, yet around every corner there is a new and more difficult challenge before me. This is brutal… mostly to my ego… All I want to do is call it quits for the day, dry off, and try again in the morning. However, being as we are on the side of a mountain, in the pouring rain with no town in sight, what other option is there but to ride on. So, I did, only confident in one thing…. I am going to die.

I am not a brand-new rider, but I am not what people would call hard core. I also do not share the wealth of experience that Charlie carries. I love traveling and I really enjoy doing it on motorcycles, but with that being said I also love taking my time to look around and to just take it all in. At this stage in my life everything about motorcycles both terrifies and excites me, yet there is no other way I would rather spend my time. The smell of the world around you, the ability to get lost in your thoughts, the sense of just being out there and vulnerable to the elements truly makes me feel alive. It is an overwhelming sensation, and quite frankly exhausting, to have white knuckling anxiety and pure exhilaration simultaneously. Everyday I woke during our overseas adventure with nervous anticipation of what sort of landscape we were getting ourselves into this time. Being from Wisconsin, (so defining myself as a flatlander), I was not as prepared for the narrow winding roads that carve in and out the European landscape. The constant twisting and turning was exhausting, and the reality of the matter is I couldn't keep up with my counterpart. Truth be told not many can, I mean he is Chopper Charlie after all.

For those that don't know me it doesn't take long to find out that I am a worrier by nature, so naturally someone with my affliction felt as if I were constantly letting him down. I had this looming feeling that he was miserable, and would have preferred to be coupled with a more experienced rider. These feelings I am fully aware were a bit on the irrational side, but also to some extent warranted. I mean there was this clue to the level of his annoyance when he literally asked me "Why do you keep falling behind, I'm not even going fast!?" as I mumbled under my breath, "Clearly fast enough to make me feel stupid…" haha…I know we love riding

Le Prese, Swizerland 5.12.15

Antwerp, Belgium 4.14.15

53

Collioure, France 5.4.15

together but I know him and I know a look on his face relates to a feeling. Many times, I looked over and I knew my anxiety was material. I had just hoped that I was projecting, but let's be real that is my best friend and I knew if I didn't step it up somehow Europe would be a disappointment to him. I would love to say these anxieties faded as the trip unfolded, but they merely dissipated slightly. I tried my best to ride like the wind as much as I possibly could and by doing so I was in a constant state of terror. I was going faster than I felt I was capable of, and I was confident I was going to meet my doom via cliff, or river, or even the friendly tree aside the road, but enough of the dramatics.

On a very real note, I was pushed beyond my limits literally every day for 7 weeks, and because I was in a constant state of learning, Charlie pushed me to be a better rider. The beauty of limits and pushing through them is it expands your ability to deal with tricky situations with more confidence as rough challenges approach. The blizzard that blinded you as you crossed that mountain pass will make that torrential downpour through the Spanish hills feel like no big deal because a little voice inside you is saying you have made it through worse. A gnarly one lane rough road along the French Mediterranean, technically the most difficult road I have had to face to date, with off camber hairpin switchback makes your typical well marked wide American switch back something manageable without a thought. The mountain road becomes something

54

to enjoy versus an impending death wish. Where there was once fear and anxiety with the question "Will I make it through that turn?", became the thought "I wonder how hard I can hit that curve." I really owe it to my partner in crime because had he gone easy on me and not pressed me to struggle, my road to enjoyment would have taken exponentially longer.

As we were rounding off toward the end of the Swiss Alps I started becoming someone not terrified of curves but someone who welcomed and even sought them out. I can vividly pin point the moment where riding made sense to me. We were in a place that screamed beauty. The Austrian Alps are bold and green and around every corner was a postcard worth taking in. We made our way through Zürs, Lech, and Warth, and something illuminated inside me. Maybe it was the sheer beauty of this place, or maybe a switch just turned on and connected my soul to my bike, but I knew I could ride as hard as I wanted. My bike started moving beneath me like a magical creature. Faster and faster I pushed on pavement of glass through quaint towns with a smile larger than I had ever imagined. Charlie at one point instinctively pulled over to wait for me after going over a pass and a look of shock took over as he realized I was right with him. I'll never forget the look on his face when we got off our motorcycles that day. He turned to me with a smile matching mine and said "Looks like someone is finally having fun!" I was, and it was the most amazing feeling one can have on the open road.

Lepe, Spain 4.28.15

Faro, Portugal 4.27.15

Alps , Switzerland 5.13.15

French Pyranese 4.24.15

Mijas, Spain 4.30.15

Mijas, Spain 4.30.15

Swiss Alps 5.13.15

Spain Portugal Boarder 4.26.15

Warth, Austria 5.14.15

INSIGHT OF THE EXPERIENCED RIDER

The experienced rider's perspective, that's what this chapter is supposed to be about and apparently, I am that guy. I've been riding for a while and HAVE seen a few things on the road, far more then Kayla, but that doesn't mean that we both didn't have our own battles to fight on this adventure. The interesting thing about riding motorcycles is that the challenges never seem to end. Every day we face new obstacles such as road conditions, weather, altitude and countless other unforeseen potential pit falls. When a rider decides to think that he has it all figured out, that is usually when a catastrophe strikes. I am a firm believer in constant growth on the road, and a European motorcycle trip through some of the worlds tightest mountains would fit my growth needs perfectly. That being said, I literally had people tell me that my long bike would never make it around many of the extremely tight switch backs Europe would dish out, that many of them would be far more extreme than what we ride on a regular basis here in Colorado. I took that as a challenge as well as with a grain of salt. Never say never. In my situation I chose to up the challenge, for reasons beyond me, and ride a motorcycle that is far from the norm. I don't know, maybe I like doing things the hard way, maybe I just like achieving what many think is unachievable. Regardless, that is how I do it and I don't foresee it changing anytime soon. I am no stranger to curvy roads, I started my motorcycling career in the motherland of curvy roads, Colorado. I am

58

also no stranger to big miles, long days, and extreme conditions, in fact I may even thrive on it. Being a bit of a mileage junky and adventure seeker, I've logged thousands of miles in rain, cold and heat. I take a bit of pride in the fact that I've ridden over roads most claim a bike like mine can't handle. I like pushing limits. Because of this I've always viewed Europe as the Holy Grail for an adventure driven motorcyclist. Between the Alps and the Pyrenees alone, there are countless roads that met my criteria of both challenging and picturesque. Tight, twisty, narrow, and reaching a high mountain pass are a few of the things that make me tick. There is no better feeling then reaching the "top" of a road.

What did this trip mean to me? What was my perspective from the so called "experienced riders" point of view? I'll tell you, it was amazing in every way, that was very much my perspective though and Kayla and I did not always see eye to eye on that. Allow me to give you an example of a situation where Kayla and I had a very different experience. It begins as we crested a tall pass somewhere in Switzerland. I forget which one exactly, as there were so many, but I will never forget the experience. As we rolled gently over the top of the mountain I could see below us the road dipping, diving, and weaving its way straight into a post card. All around us waterfalls cascaded from craggy peaks, some big, some small, as if framing the experience into a perfectly painted package. Between the curves lay a lush blanket of what seemed to be a perfectly manicured lawn. The bright green grasses lining the way and the craggy snow-covered peaks soaring high around us made it, literally, almost too good to be true. The reason why I enjoyed this so much is because I wasn't white knuckling it around every corner, I wasn't fearing for my life or concerning myself with losing control and going off the

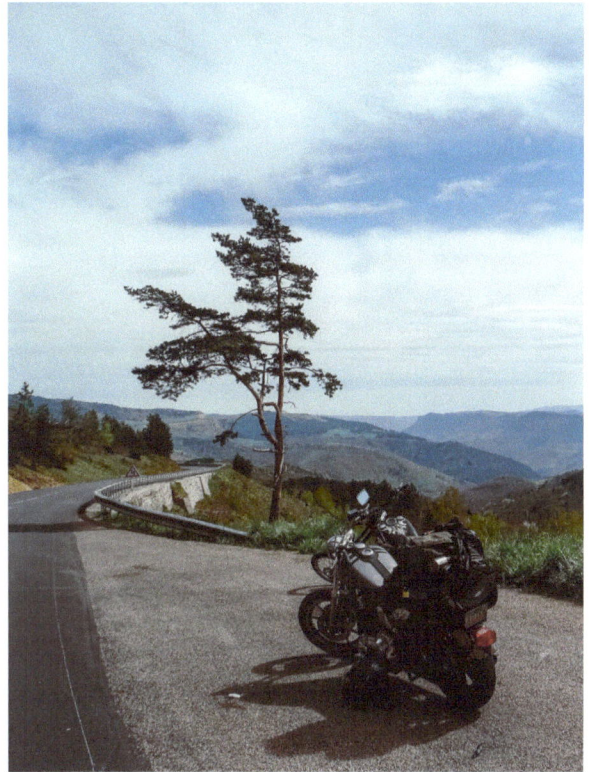

On the Road. France 4.22.15

Antwerp, Belgium 4.14.15

59

Mediteranean Sea. Barcelona, Spain 5.2.15

road, I was able to simply ride the road as it was designed to be ridden while enjoying the view around me. A situation like this is what really sets apart the perspective between an experienced rider and that of a rookie. I discovered quickly that what was exhilarating for me what was not fun at all for Kayla. Upon reaching the valley far below is when I realized how dramatic of a difference it was. I tore off my helmet, glowing with excitement, wanting to talk about how incredible it was, Kayla did not seem so pleased, but rather almost angry that I chose this particular route. It turns out that she was terrified and spent the entire ride down staring at the pavement and the upcoming curves, not the waterfalls. These are the moments when experience truly does make a difference.

It wasn't all fun and games for me though. Portugal gave me an experience that reminded me that even the most road worn motorcyclists can face everyday challenges. Albeit a rather minor moment in the trip, it was still a moment. A moment that quickly reminded me that I to have my limits. For years I've prided myself on being able to ride my incredibly long and rigid motorcycle down roads people say are unpassable on my machine. Not much of anything has stopped me in my tracks, but a roundabout, of all things, was where I found my limit. You see, we had just arrived into the picturesque town of Faro, Portugal where we were simply looking for a quiet place to park and explore the town on foot. During our quest we found ourselves approaching a dead end that was capped nicely with a relatively large roundabout. A roundabout typically would not be the sort of situation that would not be the sort of situation that would concern me, nor did this particular one at first either. The difference I quickly realized though, was that the baby head size cobblestones that paved the street posed a particularly unique problem. Difficult enough in a straight line, the cobblestones proved to be a serious challenge when attempting to make a circle, particularly on a ten-foot-long chopper. As I leaned the bike to get the turning radius required I quickly noticed that the cobblestones had a plan of their own, my long front end was no match to what they threw at me. I leaned, and I leaned further. Desperately fighting the cobblestones that seemed more interested in keeping me going in a straight line. The more I leaned the more my front wheel hopped and skipped in the opposite direction of the curve, my trajectory was now directly towards the curb about three quarters of the way through the circle. I fought and fought, trying desperately to pull the bike as far to the left as possible to avoid the curb that was now approaching quickly. It seemed the harder I pulled left, the more the cobblestones pulled me back to the right. Ultimately, I lost the battle and careened into the curb. Kayla meanwhile had successfully completed the task with seemingly no issues at all. I sat there for a second, feeling defeated. I had found my limit and it was a harsh reminder that although I may have plenty of miles under my belt, I am never finished learning. A relatively typical roundabout had now become a three-point turn for this so-called experienced rider.

There you have it, Europe from the experienced rider's point of view. Ultimately, we both had our own challenges and both learned lessons in our own way. While I was taking in the scenery, serpentining down steep, curvy passes, Kayla was learning how to pull her bike through a corner in a way that made her comfortable. Meanwhile, her suspended and normal length motorcycle handled the varying road conditions without any problems. For me it was the opposite. Paying no attention to the degree of switchbacks, I found myself wrestling old tired roads riddled with potholes, patches of cobblestone and menacing construction zones filled with deep sand. Ultimately, I would have to say that the ride was challenging for both of us, just in different ways. I for one, was reminded on multiple occasions that regardless of how many miles you may have on two wheels, there is always more to learn.

Faro, Portugal 4.27.15

Boarder Avamonte, Spain 4.28.15

Beard Cycles. Florence, Italy 5.10.15

THE ITALIANS

If there was one particular culture and people that we fell in love with I think Kayla and I would both agree that would be, without a doubt, the Italians. On so many levels we were completely impressed with the genuineness and vitality of the Italian culture, the deeply engrained sense of pride, and the desire to share that pride. Diverse, yet unified the Italians impressed us in countless ways. Finding a way to communicate our thoughts into words has proven to be difficult on this particular subject so I'd like to start by sharing one particular event we attended deep in the heart of the Italian countryside. I think it will provide some insight into what formed our opinion. It was a motorcycle campout and party unlike anything either of us had ever experienced and one that has since led to us attempting to bring the experience home with us.

If I had plugged my ears and looked around I would have bet top dollar that I was at any number of killer chopper parties here in the United States. With rebel flags flying, a staggering amount of original and chopped Harley Panheads, Knuckleheads and Flatheads, even an old heavy metal cover band, it had all the makings of a 1970's chopper mag photo reenactment...except everyone spoke Italian. I'm speaking of the Road Crew party Kayla and I attended in May 2015 near Florence, Italy. What's written in the following paragraphs isn't a run-down of every cool bike we saw (though there were plenty to choose from), or a tale of drunken debauchery (because we didn't see much of it), but more about the overall feel. An insight into how it's done across the pond and I suppose some of my own personal philosophy on what I'd like to see (and think others would like to see as well) here in the United States.

Deep in the woods of Italy, chopper enthusiasts from around the region gathered amongst three hundred some tents and motorcycles to share their love for the lifestyle. The lifestyle I'm referring to is the one that combines travel, brotherhood, family and of course, choppers. For the most part, this event was similar to the many other events we have attended with a couple of glaring differences. Differences that set this event apart from any other and differences we hope to start seeing here in US. For one, as Kayla and I stopped and looked around, we noticed that there were no clicks. You know how sometimes you roll into an event and everyone is separated into little groups based on where they stand in the chopper hierarchy? That didn't exist here. Everyone was simply there for the love of motorcycles. It didn't matter what kind of bike you were on, who you knew or what you did, they were just happy you were there. If they didn't know you, they would make the effort to introduce themselves. We watched this happen not only first hand, but all around us. Let me tell you, in a world where many seem more concerned with how they look on Instagram and Facebook, who they know and what events they are "seen" at, this was extremely refreshing. All barriers regarding social class, knowledge of motorcycles, how many miles you have under your belt, along with any other reason one might think makes them more special then the next guy, were knocked down. Call me a

Malmantile, Italy 5.9.15

Malmantile, Italy 5.9.15

Florence, Italy 5.9.15

Edolo, Italy 5.11.15

Malmantile, Italy 5.9.15

Malmantile, Italy 5.9.15

Malmantile, Italy 5.9.15

peace-loving hippy all you want, but it was damn nice to see this. Two, not only did everyone seem to be old friends (even if they weren't), but when it came time to fill their bellies everyone stopped what they were doing and lined up for a plate of pasta. Yeah, pasta, at a chopper party, a stark reminder that we were in fact still in Italy. I won't even get started on the espresso and croissants they served in the morning. After receiving their plate of spaghetti everyone proceeded to sit down, together, and enjoy a meal with friends both old and new. It was like sitting down to a meal with my family, with a little more colorful of a conversation of course. That was most certainly a first for both myself and Kayla. A family style pasta dinner, in the woods of Italy, surrounded by amazing motorcycles with some of the most genuine folks I've ever met. That's hard to beat. I realize I keep using the word family, but that's because it's the one word that truly sums up the experience. It was a zero ego, zero drama, zero bullshit environment...as it should be.

In addition to this wildly different experience the Italians had given us, their generosity continued the following morning. My bike, still plagued with starting issues, had caught the attention of the mechanics from Beard Cycles, a nearby repair and chop shop. Not allowing us to leave town without us letting them repair the annoying issue, we followed them back to their garage. There I witnessed four guys tackle the problem, find a solution and repair it in a way that still resides on my motorcycle to this day. Within two hours I was back on the road with a permanent solution that has

65

Malmantile, Italy 5.9.15

Malmantile, Italy 5.9.15

Malmantile, Italy 5.9.15

yet to fail. As soon as they were finished I pulled my wallet from my back pocket and immediately tried to pay them for their time, an offer which they refused. No matter how hard I tried they refused to take anything in return except for a photograph with Kayla and I. That is a photo we still cherish. By the time we were done fifteen more people from the party had shown up to hang out with us and offer support and help in any way they could, including Barbara and Zank who offered us a place to stay. An offer which we accepted, and has led to a lasting friendship.

We followed the couple back to their house in Vicenza where we quickly learned of their love for American culture, not limited to coffee pots and full size mugs, a far cry from your typical espresso maker and thimble sized coffee cups you would typically see in that part of the world. We spent our evening with them watching old biker movies (in English), and eating delivery pizza. The whole experience was both surreal and comforting, reminding us of home.

Barbara and Zank were just two of many people that touched our hearts in that country of fine food, incredible landscapes and an immense amount of pride for their heritage and culture. It may have been that pride, more than anything, that really stuck with us. A love for your country, so deep that you want to share it with everyone you meet, is not as common as you might think. So many people spend their lives searching for something more, something better and believing that there is a superior way of life around the corner. Not the Italians. The Italians truly believe in their hearts that they are right where they should be, and become giddy at the prospect of being able to share that with a foreigner. This excitement resonated with us and is not an experience we will soon forget.

Tarnby, Denmark 5.22.15

COLD, RAINY AND THE NORTHERN LIGHTS

This is the land of great warriors, long hard winters, and fierce Pagan gods. This is the mystic territories of the Vikings, a people driven by the gods of war and thunder in search for fertile land. These are the pagan people of Odin, Loki and Freya that struck fear and changed the face of European people. I mean they literally pillaged their way into the skirts of the fair maidens, and left their genetics all over the known world. I, being a Northwoods woman, couldn't wait to be in the Norse lands and here I was traveling through Denmark, and about to cross the bridge to Sweden to see the lands of our ancestors. I mean I'm an American mutt with mostly Northern European blood and I would say not really able to trace my ancestors back past my great grandparents, but let's be realistic I don't think many people got through the Viking era without a little bit of their blood running though their veins... especially the French and Germans. Normandy was named after the North men so I mean the facts are in the pudding. Ok.. ok.. I'm done with the history lesson and back to the adventure I swear!

We had a lot of fun putzing through Demark and trying to be more playful in our journey. We decided to get off the main drag, meander north, and find a place to stay. Our kickstands went down at the Skovland Camping in Asperup, Denmark. We set up

Bogense, Denmark 5.21.15

Stockholm, Sweden 5.24.15

Tungelsta, Sweden 5.25.15

camp and decided to take a stroll through the area. We walked through woods, did cartwheels on the coast and took time to smell the yellow flowers that were blooming all around us. We saw all these houses with thatched roofs and were astounded by how amazing they looked! When we returned to the campground we turned to see a massive fire burning in the area where we had just come from. We heard from others also watching the massive fire that the fishery was a blaze up the street, which was crazy because we were just there taking pictures. We drifted to sleep to the smell of smoke and ash.

The morning's dreary sky was no match for our excitement to be crossing The Øresund Bridge, the longest road / rail bridge in Europe. It was insane because you ride through this 2.5-mile-long underwater tunnel that turns into a five-mile bridge to cross into Sweden. After we emerged from the tunnel we very precariously pulled over to catch a shot of our bikes on the bridge. You can barely capture where we are, but I know and that's all that matters. The further north we pressed the sky darkened with menacing clouds waiting to dump their load all over us. Now we had heated gear, which always helped, but the dark gloom had a way of tricking your mind into feeling the fringed air and the dampness slowly mading its way to the core of your bones. We were headed straight to Stockholm to stay with a friend, Michail, who Charlie met on the interwebs while he was building his chopper. When we arrived, we found we were not able to stay with him but he had friends that were more than welcome to offer us their guest room, and I couldn't be happier that they did. Sussi and Richard were amazing on all fronts, they were kind and generous, possessed an epic piece of property, comforting and cozy space, and really showed us a humorous good time. They were amazing tour guides showing

68

Camping og Hytteutleie. Lindesnes, Norway 5.27.15

us all around Stockholm. The places they took us to eat were out of this world. I have never had Reindeer before and it melted in my mouth. The meal we had at Fem små hus, which translates to five small houses, was some of the most incredible savory treats I have had in my life and I'd be lying if I said I didn't leave there with the meat sweats. With a wealth of knowledge, they showed us the Bloody Square, the Palace during the changing of the guards, and some of the best places to view the city. They also shared with a bit of bitter sweetness. They felt the loss of wonder of the city due to the overfilling of immigrants who are changing their culture, and from the sound of it not for the better. We enjoyed their company so much we stayed another night to see Richards shop and just enjoy the comfort of their generosity. I so hope to see them again someday!

We headed though countless miles of rain as we crossed Sweden into Norway. Up here in the north is the first time on this trip that I truly felt unbelievable cold on the bike. Honestly, I don't remember any of my gear working, and there was self-loathing at the realization that I should never have taken off a perfectly functional front fender and replaced it with a silly bandana. We were headed to the Fjords... which we never made it to because time got the best of us, but that gives us a perfect excuse to visit this amazing region again. On this whole trip we had been crossing boarders left and

Nisser Lake, Norway 5.27.15

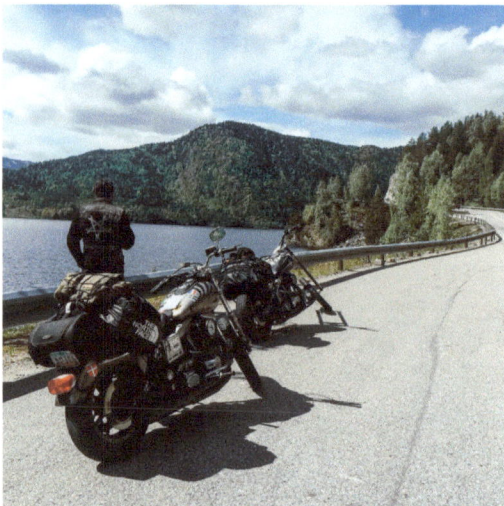
E18 on the Cost of Norway 5.26.15

E4, Sweden 5.23.15

right and crossing into Norway was the first time we had to pull out our passports and answer some questions. It was a little surreal because for the first time in a while it felt like we were in a different country. Most of our trip felt like we were passing from one state to the next. Any who we headed straight for Oslo, turned south, and stayed outside a little town called Kragero. Charlie and I stopped in the town thinking we were going to get a hotel. We decided it was a bit too expensive so we took a stroll to figure out if we could try to find camping, and that's when it happened. Charlie in a panic almost shit himself, squatting at the side of the road using all his constitution to keep his faculties intact. I couldn't stop laughing, but he was enraged with fear. With a deep breath, he waddled back to the hotel where he unloaded in the public restroom. Which wasn't a big deal, but then we just got on our motorcycles and left. I mean who does that? Show interest in a room, use their private parking, destroy the bathroom for about 20 minutes and just bounce without making a single purchase. What jerks! We found a lovely quiet camping spot only a few miles away!

The next day we backtracked a bit up to Skein, and over to Kviteseid so we could ride a scenic road. 41 south to 42 and over to the southernmost town of Norway called Lindesnes. It was at this point we realized that time was no longer on our side and we were not going to be able to make it north to the Fjords, so we tried to make the most of what time we had to experience a little bit of Norway. Other than some construction, and a massive detour that had us completely turned around, the road was epically beautiful. I think Charlie and I stopped about 40 times to take in the views. Charming towns, massive lakes, mountains, winding roads, and enormous hills as a backdrop. Norway really impressed us, and we had no idea there was so much amazing

70

Solplassen Camping AS. Stavern, Norway 5.26.15

beauty up here. Maybe I was a little naive because I think of these places and I just think of snow, but it was very lush and brilliant green.

Camping for the night in Camping og Hytteutleie in Lindesnes was one of the most amazing nights of our trip in my opinion. We pitched the tent overlooking the sea, and took an amazing walk along the coast to take it all in. We hunted jellyfish and lady bugs in and among the rocks. We stumbled upon a dock where we sat for a couple of hours watching the waves being pushed ashore by the whipping wind. I felt there was something nostalgic about this night, mainly because this was the final turning point in our journey that would take us back to where we began. From this point we would turn the bikes back to Belgium. We closed our eyes to the sound of the wind howling past our tent. A storm was coming.

As we wiped the sleep from our eyes the rain was coming down pretty good. Nothing worse that packing up wet gear because now everything in your bag was going to be soaked for the remainder of the day. It was time to make our way back south and into Denmark, but to do so required ferry travel from Kristiansand to Hirtshal. We stopped for coffee a few miles from camp hoping maybe the rain would calm, but the down pour didn't let up. We wanted to catch the early ferry, so we sucked it up and took the winding coast road to the port. I don't know which was more miserable, the

Norway to Denmark Ferry 5.28.15

Norway to Denmark Ferry 5.28.15

Lindesnes, Norway 5.27.15

ride or waiting in line drenched with a few other motorists from Germany for what seemed like hours. They finally opened the gates and we followed the assembly line through twists and turns onto the dock. I have experienced some eerie things on a bike, but man is it crazy riding onto the ship with wet slick metal below you while the ship rocks back and forth. I remember the ship rocking, and me sliding into a spot and saying, "well I'm parking here." ha-ha. Charlie glared with annoyance as his bike wasn't really fitting in the allotted spaces for motorists. Actually, compared to the other bikes, I believe Charlie's back wheel was completely outside the little yellow lines that designated the spots. We strapped down the bikes best we could, crossed our fingers that they would stay put, and made our way to the seating deck. We sat down thinking eh, it's just a ferry there is no way Charlie would get sick like he did when we were crossing the Atlantic, but we couldn't be more wrong. As that ship started moving Charlie ran straight for the bathroom where he stayed for pretty much the duration of crossing the Skagerrak. He was so green I didn't know if he was even going to be able to ride his bike off the boat. But he got it off and we literally made it two miles to the first hotel. We stayed for the night so he could recover. We also desperately needed to dry our clothing and gear that was smelling pretty moldy at this point. Our room looked and reeked like a hobo camp in 90-degree heat. A least we were dry and Charlie was finally starting to get color back in his skin!

Soldeu, Andorra 4.24.15

CRIOSSANTS, CAMPFIRES AND COUSINE

If the kitchen is the heart of the home, then food is one of the biggest joys of travel. It is around the simple act of eating where we connect with one another, and divulge the experiences of the day. Our friends across the pond truly have made the enjoyment of eating an art form. Even the simplest cup of coffee is served as an aesthetic display of perfection. Every country or region you travel to you are entering a new cultural realm of culinary treats, and I was tickled with excitement. From campfires to fine dining we enjoyed the best food Western Europe has to offer.

Most mornings Charlie and I would start the day with bread or a pastry either fresh from the bakery or "carefully" rolled in a maze of napkins from the day before. This Euro tradition of pastry making dates back to ancient times… it's fact don't argue… and their simple, flakey perfection is evidence of the hundreds of years it took to perfect them. Although we tried several different styles and types, the fact that Charlie and I have massive sweet tooth's which may have influenced our personal favorite, which was the buttery croissant filled with rich chocolate, and drizzled with more rich chocolate, yet it wasn't too sweet making it more awesome. The glaring difference we noticed between the American and the European pastry was the overall sweetness. The

CT El Guijo. Salamanca, Spain 4.26.15

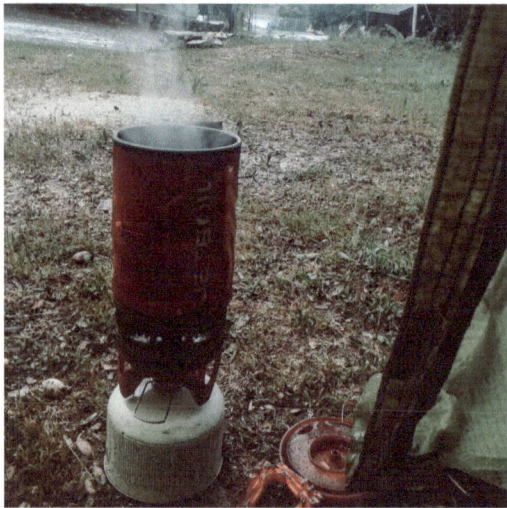

CT El Guijo. Salamanca, Spain 4.26.15

First meal on the Atlantic 4.3.15

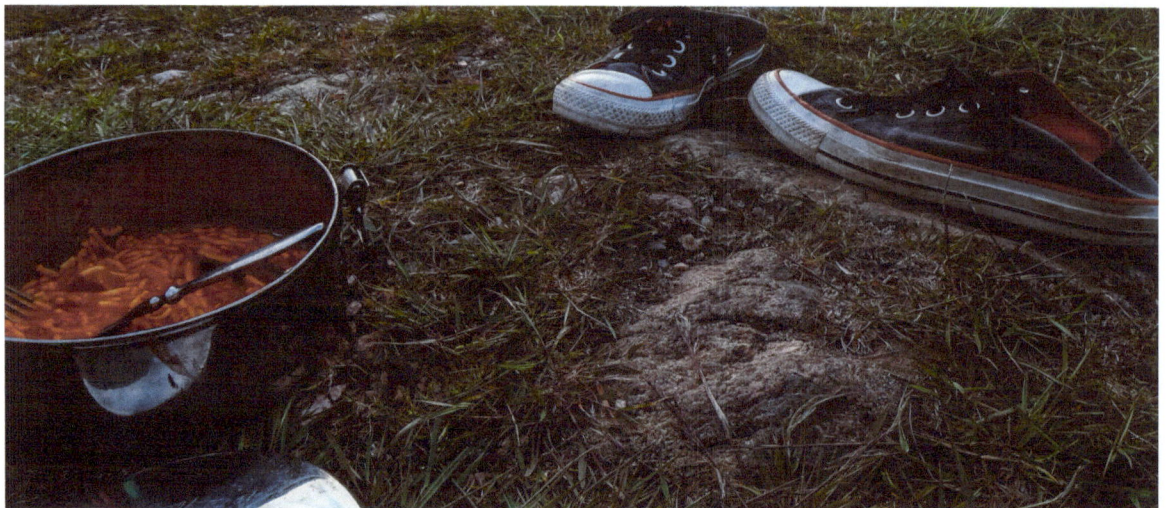

Camping og Hytteutleie. Lindesnes, Norway 5.27.15

European treat was flakey, which makes it ridiculously messy, and if you are new to this will make you look equally ridiculous when you eat in front of people, but it was light with a delicate balance of sweetness that left you happily satisfied. The American pastry on the other hand has a tendency to be dense and covered in glazes, making for a cleaner experience yet also forcing you feel as if you are moments from plummeting into a diabetic coma. Those few moments of "Sweetness System Overload" are vastly overshadowed by the hours of general nausea and discomfort. So, I guess what I'm saying is I wish we had light pastries at home because I would enjoy eating them more often.

You know what goes amazing with pastries? You nailed it. Coffee. I'm not going to lie coffee is one of the greatest loves of my life. I don't drink…anymore… I don't smoke, I don't do drugs, so I will have all the coffee I want and try to stop me. I like it from a French press, I like it in all forms of espresso cocktails, and I even like it from the drip if done right and, well Europe does it all right. I have never had a coffee in Europe where I had the thought "Ugh that tastes burnt" or "I think you forgot the chocolate in my mocha…". It is just joy from the moment it is served. The presentation, which is catching on in the United states, is always different with a flare of uniqueness that I tend to place as equally important as the taste itself. Nothing sets the mood of pleasure better than an attractive display. Sometimes there is a biscotti, or a chocolate bar, or even a unique chunk of sugar, but no matter what the extra embellishments are they all do the same thing; puts a smile on your face before you even dive into the main course. So now you have doctored it up, taken in her beautiful smell, and let that first taste cross your lips. A sigh of relaxed delight escapes as you take it all in. You are left looking at people passing by, the person

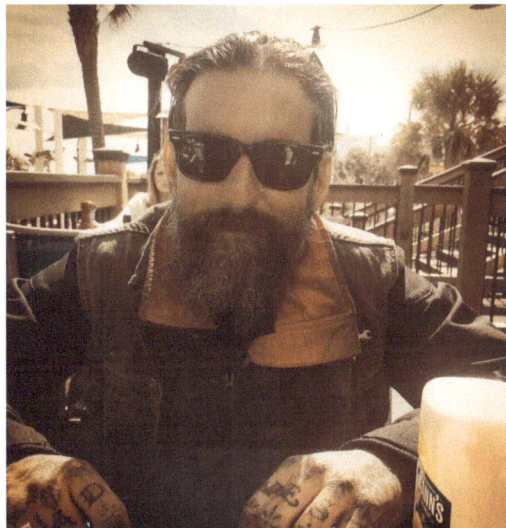

Myrtle Beach, South Carolina 3.25.15

Amsterdam, Netherlands 6.5.15

Barcelona, Spain 5.2.15

Nothing like European Coffee. Antwerp, Belgium 6.1.15

with you, and thinking life doesn't get much better than this. That's enough talking about something I'm clearly addicted to, and let us dive into the meat and potatoes.

When it comes to trying food, I will eat almost anything, but Charlie literally will eat everything (now whether or not he is able to keep it down is another story). Seriously, that man throws up more than anyone I know…aaand he should probably get that checked out. Most of our lunches were grabbed from a petrol stop, or a quick road side lunch, but our dinners is where we really indulged. There were three main ways we would spend our evening meals which included cooking at our campsite, eating at the homes of the new and exciting people we met on the road, and finally eating local fare.

We had little travel plans so our plan for food really depended on where we were going to sleep that night. If it appeared we would be tenting it, to conserve our dough for gasoline, we would stop by a small market to collect the items to make dinner. We would grab local dried meats, olives, unique cheeses, fruit, and fresh baked bread. Essentially, we made a feast of charcuterie and cheese plates. Occasionally, I would let Charlie pick the main course for the campground, not that he has bad taste he just never seems overly enthused making decisions when he doesn't have to. This is how, against my protests and warnings, we ended up eating canned spaghetti at a campground in Norway. He hadn't been feeling well that day so I let him pick whatever he wanted…. mistake… The spaghetti was, as one would imagine, a gelatinous mess that tasted like it was canned with dirty feet. Charlie ran to edge of the clearing to throw up causing him to feel even worse, and I'm the one with the iron stomach who almost threw up but what were we going to do that was the only food we had for the night.

A more enjoyable means of eating was with the countless friends who invited us into their homes to dine with them. Overwhelmed and overjoyed by too many courses with our friends Jean and Elizabeth. I remember eating and filling up and then hearing the words "Are you ready for the main course? Don't forget to save room for desert,"...whoops. The breakfast spread our friends Sussi and Richard put together in Sweden was one of my favorite things to wake up to. From sliced meats and cheeses, to boiled eggs topped with fish eggs, to fruits and coffee, they had everything one could need. We enjoyed BBQs, pasta, and even delivery pizza (in Italy which seemed odd) in many homes all over the EU.

Lastly local fare and fine dining as it was meant to be. We treated ourselves by dining out as much as we could. There were some embarrassing moments, such as ordering steak in France or wiener schnitzel in Austria. We felt like idiots because steak in France is basically a hamburger without a bun and well we both though schnitzel was a sausage...ugh... But all embarrassment aside we had a four-course meal in Barcelona ending in filet mignon, wild game in Sweden that you never imagined would taste so magical, paella in Spain, curried ketchup in Germany, sardines in Collioure, whole squid in Portugal, and of course pasta in Italy. We walked into a place to have dinner in Hamburg that was straight out of an 80's mafia movie, but the best meals were the ones shared with buddies. You would need a whole series of novels to express the culinary experience, of this trip but I'll leave you with this; I would eat my way through Europe for the rest of my days in full and utter bliss.

Serpa, Portugal 4.27.15

Charleston, South Carolina 5.27.15

Collioure, France 5.4.15

Elizabeth, New Jersey 8.7.15

THE JOURNEY HOME

Why we thought the end of our adventure would be any less interesting then the beginning is beyond me. It seems like we should know better by this point then to think that recovering our motorcycles from a customs warehouse in New Jersey would be anything but simple. By the time we received word that our bikes were ready to be picked up we had been back in the United States for nearly three weeks, in which time we had begun to integrate ourselves back into our typical routines of work and house chores, certainly not anything worth writing about. Upon receiving that long-awaited call, we knew that our European excursion was officially about to come to a close, but not without one final cross country ride to cap it off.

Within a couple of days of that phone ringing we had purchased plane tickets for a flight to the Newark Airport, and began packing our gear for the 1,800-mile ride back to Colorado. Packing for a motorcycle ride that starts with a plane ride poses certain challenges but we managed to sort it out and were soon on our way. Newark, New Jersey isn't exactly a destination city for world travelers, but it is a major shipping port with countless warehouses filled to the brim with all sorts of goods. Inside one of these warehouses sat our motorcycles in a condition that was unknown to us. Last time we saw them they were sitting parked on their side stands in Antwerp, Belgium. We literally had no idea how, or if, they were crated, or simply parked in a corner someplace. It turns out that they were crated, if you want to call the Fort Knox of wood boxes a crate. I'm not sure if the fabricator of our crates had a surplus of nails, or maybe got paid by the number of nails used, but I can assure you that they were quite possibly the most secure motorcycle shipping crates ever built. Also keep in mind that we showed up without tools and managed to only find one child size hammer to borrow from one of the employees on site. For two hours we hammered and clawed our way into these boxes, basically beating the living hell out of them until we could start ripping them apart like barbarians, and eventually found our bikes nestled securely inside. Issue number two was that the fuel tanks were completely empty, so we trekked the couple of miles to the nearest gas station (and possibly the nations sketchiest), to purchase a gallon of fuel and a fuel can from the man behind bullet proof glass and steel bars. We only needed enough fuel to get us back to that particular gas station and then we could finally be on our way.

West bound, we began our final ride back to the reality of home life. These rides, the ones where you point your front wheel in the direction of home, are always the most difficult. Rides that are filled with all sorts of emotions ranging from a sense of accomplishment, to a sadness from the realization that the journey is almost over, and everything in between. This time though I think Kayla and I were both more focused on what we had accomplished. Nearly three months on the road through 16 European countries, two crossings of the United States, and more memories than could be put into words. We crossed the Swiss Alps and the Atlantic Ocean. We weaved through the Black Forest of Germany and watched the midnight sun in Sweden. We stared at Africa from the Rock of Gibraltar and met friends that will remain friends forever. This trip proved to be difficult, rewarding, and enlightening in every way and will prove itself to be just one of many more.

Elizabeth, New Jersey 7.8.15

Antwerp, Belgium. 6.2.15

Antwerp, Belgium. 6.1.15

More about the Authors

Visit Instagram and Follow
@RoadsareforJourneys and @CharlieTravelingChopper

Or Visit
InfernoArtStudio.com

See you on the Road.

www.ingramcontent.com/pod-product-compliance
Lightning Source LLC
Chambersburg PA
CBHW042021080426
42735CB00003B/131